U-111 Exposed is a factual account of the career of the German U-boat *U-111*: a book that consists entirely of documented evidence and first-hand accounts that led to a remarkable discovery that no one wanted to believe was possible: a long-lost U-boat that was found at a depth where it was not supposed to be.

The truth is now exposed.

This book is about a missing U-boat from the Great War: its background, its discovery, its location, and its eventual identification.

I know so much about the *U-111* because I first started researching it in the 1980's. When I learned from official documents that it lay at a depth of 266 fathoms, or 1,596 feet, I put it aside. It 1989, when Ken Clayton and I formulated the Billy Mitchell Wrecks Project, I brought the *U-111* out of hibernation. Even though I could not dive to such a depth, I included it with the Billy Mitchell chapter in *Shipwrecks of Virginia* (1992).

The BMW-Project continued throughout the 1990's, starting with our discovery of and dive on the German battleship *Ostfriesland*, at a depth of 380 feet, until we located and dived on eight of the nine German warships that were scuttled by naval gunnery, and by aerial bombardment from Billy Mitchell's nascent air force.

The only exclusion was the *U-111*. Yet since then, the errant U-boat has re-entered the limelight, due in no small part to my continued research and keen observation.

The truth is now exposed, and I am in the prime position to publish its saga. I am the acknowledged expert on sunken U-boats and submarines, not only because I have discovered, identified, and dived on three U-boats and one American submarine, but also because I have written about them and dozens of other sunken U-boats and Allied submarines around the globe.

Now I have written a detailed and truthful recounting of the *U-111* against the background of its sister boats, so that my readers will understand how and why they are located in deep water off the coast of Virginia.

This book is not fictitious hype. It is a true report. It is history.

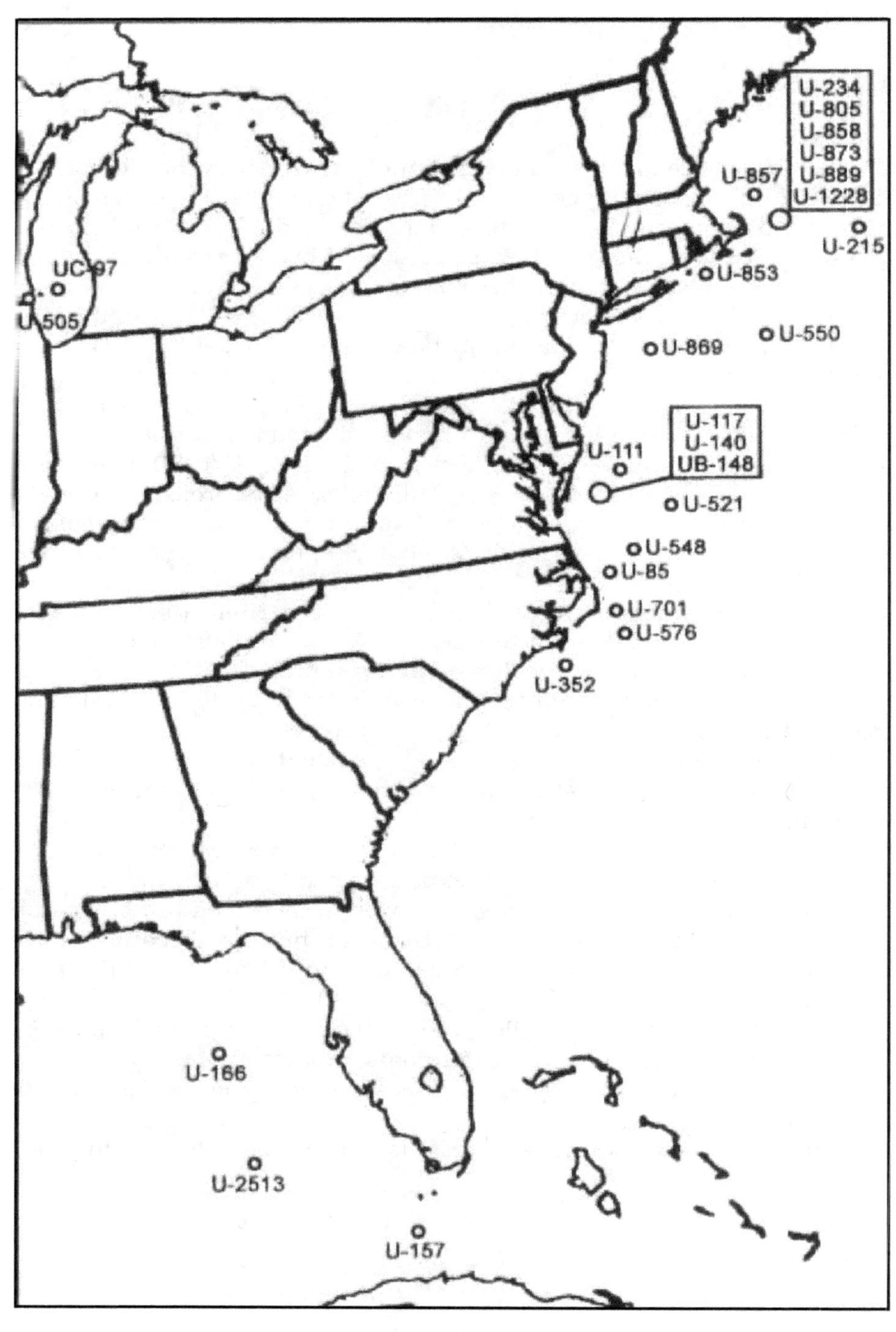
U-234
U-805
U-858
U-873
U-889
U-1228
U-857
U-215
U-853
UC-97
U-505
U-550
U-869
U-117
U-140
UB-148
U-111
U-521
U-548
U-85
U-701
U-576
U-352
U-166
U-2513
U-157

U-111 EXPOSED

The Truth About its Discovery, Identification, and Treachery

by Gary Gentile

The chart image on the left shows the place where I marked the location of the *U-111*, which I took from the *Falcon's* deck log circa 1989 to 1992. The numbers approximate the depth in fathoms (1 fathom = 6 feet). The faint tan and turquoise lines represent loran-A time delays. The chart image on the right shows the date of the chart's edition. I purchased this chart in the mid- to late-1970's, for use with my shipwreck research, which eventually developed into my Popular Dive Guide Series about shipwrecks off the eastern seaboard of the United States.

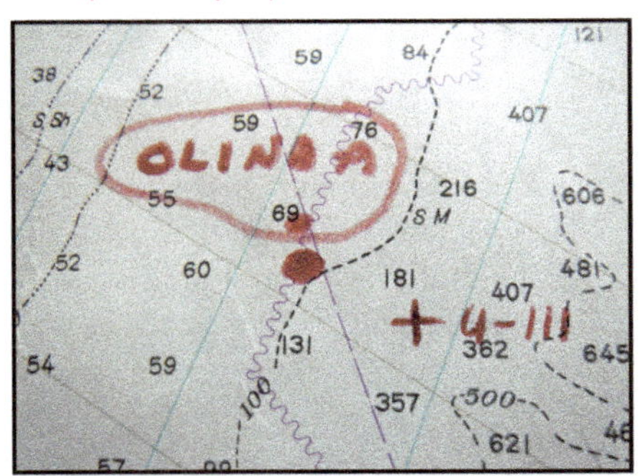

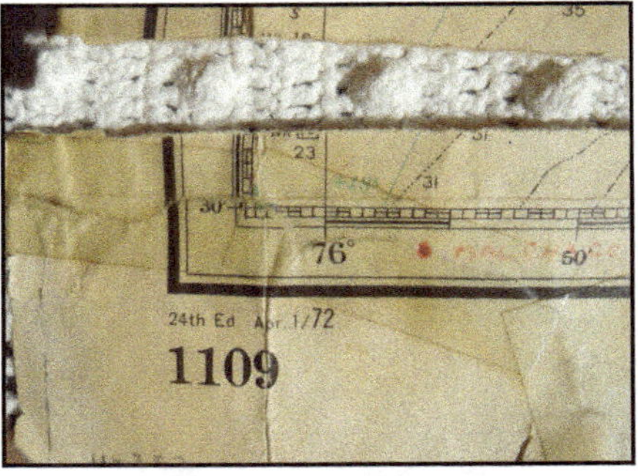

GPS co-ordinates for the *U-111*: 37-47.268 / 74-11.873

Gary Gentile Productions

Gary Gentile Productions
500 Lehigh Gorge Drive
Jim Thorpe, PA 18229

Additional copies of this book may be purchased from the same address by sending a check or money order in the amount of $20 U.S. for each copy (plus $4 postage per order, not per book, in the U.S. Inquire for shipping cost to foreign countries). Alternatively, copies may be ordered from the author's website and paid by credit card:

http://www.ggentile.com

Picture Credits
The front cover image is courtesy of the Naval Photographic Center. The back cover top photograph is from the author's collection. The back cover bottom photograph is courtesy of the Naval Photographic Center. All uncredited photographs were taken by the author.

The author would like to express his personal thanks to Ben Roberts, not only for his side-scan sonar images but also for his archival documentation relevant to the *R-8* and *Olinda*; and to Ross Baxter for his underwater video footage. Without their contributions in corroborating the identity of the *U-111*, this book could not have been as conclusive as it is.

International Standard Book Numbers (ISBN)
1-883056-61-6
978-1-883056-61-2

First Edition

Printed in U.S.A.

CONTENTS

Introduction

For me, the search for the *U-111* began in the late 1980's. That is when I started working earnestly on my Popular Dive Guide Series. The first book in the series was *Shipwrecks of New Jersey*, which was published in 1988. By now (2022), there are seventeen books in the series, covering shipwrecks from Maine to Georgia and in the Chesapeake Bay.

Researching all these shipwrecks was a monumental task. I conducted the vast majority of this research in Washington, DC (District of Columbia): the seat of the United State government and the holding facilities for a number of archival resources such as the National Archives, the Naval Historical Center, the U. S. Coast Guard Historian's Office, and the Judge Advocate General.

I commenced my shipwreck research in the 1970's by taking a day off work and driving to Washington with fellow shipwreck researcher Eric Garay. I left my house in Northeast Philadelphia at oh dark hundred, drove for an hour to Eric's house in Media, then transferred to his car for the additional two-hour trip to DC. Typically, he dropped me and my copy stand at the back door of the National Archives, after which he searched for a place to park the car. We did archival research all day until closing time, then drove home. We shared our research findings with each other.

After I retired from my job as an electrician, and became a fulltime author, in 1979, I visited local museums and libraries in the States where I was researching offshore sites. My research trips took me all along the eastern seaboard.

In the 1980's, it was my good fortune to meet fellow diver Dave Bluett when he organized dive trips to North Carolina. Dave lived in Vienna, Virginia on the outskirts of DC. He was not a researcher, but because we were dive buddies, he let me stay at his house any time I wanted. This enabled me to conduct week-long research trips, which I did many times a year for the next thirty years. From his house I either took the Metro train into DC, or drove my vehicle to the out-of-town facilities.

Throughout my life, I estimate that I've spent about one full year doing shipwreck research in Washington. This does not count research that I've done in other locations. And that is only one third of the work.

Another third is surveying shipwrecks along the east coast and in the Great Lakes. I've made more than 2,500 dives, and have spent more than three years at sea in order to make those dives.

The last third is the time that it takes to do the actual writing.

Do not make the mistake of thinking that books write themselves. It's hard work with very little reward: monetary or otherwise. I made far more money by working as an electrician.

Preparatory to writing *Shipwrecks of Virginia*, I conducted a massive amount of research both in the archives and under water. One subject

General Billy Mitchell.
(Courtesy of the National Archives.)

that interested me greatly was General Billy Mitchell and what I call the Billy Mitchell Wrecks: eleven ex-German warships which the U.S. government appropriated after the end of World War One: the giant battleship *Ostfriesland*, the cruiser *Frankfort*, the destroyers *G-102*, *S-132*, *V-43*, and six U-boats: *U-111*, *U-117*, *U-140*, *UB-88*, *UB-148*, and *UC-97*.

After U.S. Navy engineers conducted exacting studies of these vessels, their equipment, and their operations, they were slated to be scuttled by the terms of the Naval Limitation Treaty by no later than August 9, 1921. This arms limitation treaty was enforced by the Allied nations. The treaty allowed nations to own and operate a specific amount of warship tonnage, including Germany, except that Germany was not permitted to possess or build U-boats - thanks to the efforts of Great Britain's tireless leader, Winston Churchill.

In 1988, I had another good fortune. This was when I met Ken Clayton on a dive trip to Key West, Florida, where we dived on the U.S. cruiser *Wilkes-Barre*, which lay at a depth of 250 feet. Ken was fascinated by deep-water shipwrecks.

Coincidentally, I met him again later that year when I gave a slide presentation to Capital Divers, in the DC area. Because of the presentation, I picked that week to spend doing research in Washington. Before the presentation, Ken pulled me aside and showed me a picture of a ship on which he wanted to dive: the *Ostfriesland*. Ironically, I had spent most of that very day researching the Billy Mitchell Wrecks in general, and the *Ostfriesland* in particular. I opened my briefcase and showed him some of my photocopies.

We talked after the presentation. Because of our mutual interest, we decided to work together by sharing the results of our research, and by looking for ways to locate and dive on the Billy Mitchell Wrecks.

The incomplete *Washington*. (Courtesy of the Library of Congress.)

In 1989, we located and dived on the scuttled U.S. battleship *Washington* at a depth of 290 feet. On the bottom, both of us were badly affected by nitrogen narcosis. From that dive we learned that we could

The German battleship *Ostfriesland*. Note the American flag on the mast. (Courtesy of the Naval Photographic Center.)

Ostfriesland top and bottom.
(Both photos on this page are courtesy of the Naval Photographic Center.)

not explore the *Ostfriesland* while breathing air. We had to breathe a mixture of oxygen and helium. And that meant that we had to develop a whole new system of decompressing in the open ocean.

In 1990, we found and dived on the *Ostfriesland.* The depth was 380 feet. We then spent the next six years systematically locating and diving on the rest of the Billy Mitchell Wrecks. Our deepest dive was on the *Frankfurt*, which lies at a depth of 420 feet. For more details, read Book Two of *The Lusitania Controversies*. These volumes are not about only the *Lusitania* – both a history of the ship and of the history-making dives on the *Lusitania* (at a depth of 300 feet) – they incorporate a history of wreck-diving and its growth and evolution, as well as a personal biography of my involvement in deep wreck-diving and my initiation of technical mixed-gas diving, which enabled divers to reach such depths on scuba.

We also discovered and dived on the remaining warships, including all three U-boats that were part of the scuttling program. I think that it is pertinent for me to reprint what I have already written about these German U-boats: first, an introductory article that I wrote for a magazine called *Sub Aqua Journal* (1997), then reprinted in *Shipwreck Sagas* (2008); second, an extract from Book Two of *The Lusitania Controversies* (1999); third, a chapter from *The Kaisers U-boats in American Waters* (2010). And fourth, individual chapters about each U-boat from *Shipwrecks of Virginia* (1992), by which time of publication the only U-boat that we had discovered was the *U-140*.

"Diving the Kaiser's U-boats"

At a depth of 200 feet, the cerulean blue water below showed no sign of ending. I raised my eyebrows at my buddy, Ken Clayton. He shrugged. The current was strong, and my arms were feeling the strain of the pull down the anchor line. We paused for a moment to rest. It wasn't good to get out of breath at depth, so we paced ourselves accordingly. We didn't know how deep we had to go to touch the wreck that we hoped lay silently on the bottom.

At 210 feet the water continued greenish blue and featureless. At 220 it was the same. At 230 I began to see a dim ghostly outline. At 240 the shadowy shape took on definite form. It was the hull of a sunken ship.

Ambient light visibility was nearly 50 feet, the result of Gulf Stream intrusion which sometimes brushed the offshore waters of Virginia. At 250 feet I could see the hull distinctly. The side facing us rose vertically to an upper edge that curved back to form the deck; the plating was remarkably well preserved. The thinly encrusted metal cast little reflected light, and the overall dull gray was mottled with splotches of lighter shades in a nearly monochromatic design.

What I could see of the wreck so far looked very much like a submarine.

My exhilaration turned to anxiety when I saw that the grapnel had not hooked the hull, but the sand!

The grapnel had dragged over the top of the wreck, fallen to the white sandy bottom on the down-current side, and snagged with a single tine on something that lay completely buried. With a viselike grip on the anchor line in case the grapnel suddenly came free, I dropped to the sand to examine the stability of the hook.

Although only one tine had caught, it was gripped firmly on the edge of a thick steel plate only a foot from where the hull met the sand. No matter how hard I twisted and yanked, I could not move the grapnel – and the boat up above to which it was secured – against the force of the current. I raised my eyebrows at Ken, who hovered above me and oversaw my actions. He nodded.

I let go of the line. Instinctively I felt behind my tanks for my decompression reel, just in case. My depth gauge registered 266 feet. We kicked upward and alighted upon the deck about fifteen feet above the bottom. What looked like the end extended to our left, so we went right.

In just a minute or two we reached an upthrust structure that was distinctly discernible as a conning tower. And not the conning tower of an American sub, but a German U-boat.

And not just any U-boat, but a World War *One* U-boat.

Specifically, the *U-140*.

Courtesy of the Naval Photographic Center.

Germany launched a deadly U-boat offensive against the American eastern seaboard in 1918. During a six-month spree, half a dozen U-boats spread death and destruction among neutral and allied merchant shipping, sail and steam, resulting in the loss of more than one hundred vessels, including the U.S. armored cruiser *San Diego*. These U-boats laid mines along shipping lanes and in harbor approaches, shelled unarmed merchantmen, placed bombs in the holds of captured vessels and set their crews adrift, and torpedoed ships without warning – all as part of the Kaiser's bid to dominate the world.

The *U-140* accounted for seven of these shipping losses, totaling 30,594 tons. Now the Hun lies in an unmarked grave in the same ocean where its victims lie equally unmarked.

The discovery of the *U-140* was part of a long-term deep-water project which Ken and I initiated in 1989. In that year, after six aborted attempts, we reached the site of the U.S. battleship *Washington*. Although the wreck lay 290 feet deep, we conducted the dive on air, lulled deeper than we anticipated because of the deceptive reading on the boat's depth recorder, and by visibility that can only be described as seductive.

After that dive we decided to get technical. No mixed gas training programs existed at the time – the phrase "technical diving" had not yet come into vogue – so we learned "on the job" how to take a high-tech diving operation on the road, or, more accurately, on the ocean. We followed the advice of experienced cave divers who breathed mixed gas on deep underground penetrations. We adapted their techniques where appropriate, and invented our own to meet the uncontrolled conditions of the open-ocean environment. These initiatives enabled us to dive on the German battleship *Ostfriesland* on mixed gas – but that's another story. This chapter is about U-boats.

Both Ken and I curried the favor of fishing boat captains who shared with us their "hang" logs. A hang log is a list of coordinates – loran or GPS numbers – on which commercial trawling vessels have "hung" or snagged their nets. In order to avoid losing additional expensive gear, trawler captains maintained records of nasty places to shun. Most hangs are boulders, ledges, or geological outcrops. About one in ten is a shipwreck.

The next U-boat on our discovery agenda was the *UB-148*. According to our historical documentation, the wreck lay close to the *U-140* in about the same depth. We had promising numbers. On a subsequent trip, we anchored into the *U-140* for the benefit of those who hadn't dived it before. The rest of us saved our surface interval and waited to dive the "new" U-boat – hoping, of course, that we could find it.

Chris Stone went down alone. When he returned, Mike Hillier, captain of the *Miss Lindsey*, couldn't get the grapnel out. Stone bounced down and cut the tines free from the net in which they were snagged. Afterward, listening to Stone describing the wreck, Ken and I had a creepy feeling that either he had been narked the whole time despite breathing mixed gas, or . . .

. . . Hillier had gotten the numbers mixed up and took us to the wrong coordinates. Thus Chris Stone made not only the first dive on the *UB-148*, but the first two dives!

With the wreck rehooked, Ken and I dived separately and alone, although our paths crossed several times on the bottom and on the anchor line: characteristic wreck-diving buddy technique. Thirty feet of ambient light graced the bottom, but I cringed when I saw how tenuous the grapnel was set: it had caught in a twisted knot of netting that was stretched taught to a point some fifteen feet off a break in the hull. The strain of the boat prevented me from budging the grapnel to reset it in metal. When I examined the net closely, I saw with relief that within the mass of rope and twine a thick steel cable lay embedded. I went exploring.

About twenty feet of the bow had been blown off, exposing two long bronze torpedo tubes, one of which lay almost completely free and appeared to be easily recoverable. The ten-foot gap between the forward compartment and the pressure hull was knitted together by the net in which the grapnel was hooked. The wreck sat upright, and the shell of the conning tower rose about eight above the rusting deck. Twenty feet off the port side of the conning tower, a string of buoys floated a net off the bottom like a thick lace curtain suspended from rods. Abaft the conning tower on top of the hull gaped a hole the size of a double door. I should have been able to peer into the engine room, but the interior was filled with sand and silt to within three feet of the rim.

The depth to the bottom was 274 feet.

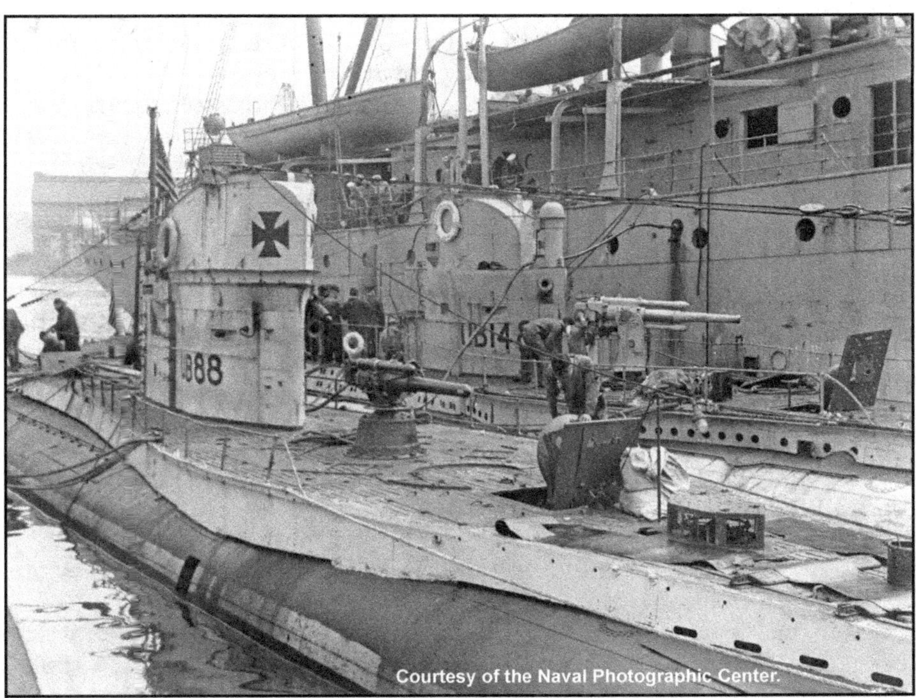

Courtesy of the Naval Photographic Center.

The damage sustained by both U-boats was inflicted by naval shellfire, not as a casualty of war but as part of a gunnery test.

After the cessation of hostilities, a small fleet of German warships was brought to the United States as war reparations: six U-boats, three destroyers, a cruiser, and a battleship. The U-boats became tourist attractions after all eleven warships were examined minutely by naval engineers. Then they were all scuttled in accordance with the terms of the Naval Limitation Treaty.

One U-boat was scuttled off the California coast, another in Lake Michigan, yet a third in deep water off the Atlantic continental shelf.

None has ever been dived. The remaining U-boats and warships were put down in an area known as the Southern Drill Grounds, which is where we found them. Their disposal was not wasted.

In 1921, Brigadier General Billy Mitchell set out to prove to the world at large, and to the U.S. Navy in particular, that warships had lost the supremacy of the sea that they had enjoyed since man's early conflicts. Capital ships had been superseded by a recent invention: the airplane. He proposed to demonstrate the concept of airborne superiority by bombing warships from the air. The German relics served his purposes admirably.

The *U-140* and the *UB-148* were shelled by surface vessels, but the *U-117* was sunk by aerial bombardment from Billy Mitchell's planes. The reason we looked for the *U-117* last, despite its importance in our overall quest to dive those particular vessels that were sunk by Mitchell's bombers, was a function of progressive depth exploration. Naval records indicated that the *U-117* went down where the water was 300 feet deep. We were working our way down, so to speak.

From historical accounts we chose the most probable location and correlated it with the hang numbers that we had in the area. After hours of searching with no result, we resignedly moved off site to check out another set of numbers nearby, but only 230 feet deep. Any unexplored wreck could be interesting.

This time we got lucky and found the numbers right on target. Ken Clayton and Peter Hess went down first. Just as they began their ascent the grapnel pulled out and the boat went adrift, so the rest of us had to wait out their decompression before entertaining the possibility of a dive. When they finally surfaced, we were as astonished as they to learn that the wreck was that of a submarine!

I knew of three U.S. submarines that had been scuttled off the Virginia coast, and concluded that we must have stumbled onto one of them. When we rehooked, the anchor chain fell across the edge of the conning tower, which I studied in detail without observing anything that provided clues to the sub's identity. Dark, dismal conditions prevailed on the bottom, almost like a night dive. I didn't stray far.

For two years we agonized over which sub it could be. Then we returned on a day when visibility exceeded fifty feet ambient. I took a grand tour from end to end. It was immediately obvious how the wreck's location became known: the towing yokes of two trawler rigs, expensive shipwreck locator devices, were firmly implanted in the starboard hull.

Not until I examined the stern carefully and compared my drawing with historical photos did I recognize the distinctive slope as the after deck above the minelaying tubes. It was the *U-117* all along, misplaced by both leagues and fathoms.

Through those tubes once slid the mines that sank the *Chaparra* and the *San Saba* off the New Jersey coast, the *Saetia* off Maryland, and the *Mirlo* off North Carolina. Through one of the tubes in the bow sped the torpedo that sank the *Sommerstad* off Long Island's southern

A post card picture of the *U-117* from the author's collection.

shore, in that long ago August when war raged over the world.

There is more to behold and explore on these wrecks than I have seen for myself or described. They are three of a kind, if you will, together comprising a rare insight into Germany's first undersea and most effective killing machine, and the precursor of deadly events to come a generation later.

To dive on the Kaiser's U-boats is to touch the heart of history. They are waiting for you silently. Go see them.

This print in the author's collection shows the bombing of the *U-117*. Note the three observation vessels in the photograph, and the three bi-wing aircraft (biplanes) toward the upper left part of the frame, below the words "the frame" in this sentence.

The Lusitania Controversies (Book Two) German U-boat Discoveries

In addition to the German warships situated at extraordinary depths, we [Ken Clayton and I] also conducted a parallel series of historic wreck discoveries: the U-boats that were sunk in the 1921 bombing tests. In 1992 we located the *U-140* at a depth of 266 feet, and the *UB-148* at 274 feet. These were the first U-boats of World War One vintage ever dived in American waters.

The following year we found the *U-117* at 233 feet. We didn't identify it at first because it wasn't where it was supposed to be, and because of the inky blackness on the bottom. I mistook it for a possible scuttled American sub, although Clayton had his suspicions. Not until 1995 did I identify the U-boat to my satisfaction. I did it by comparing features on the wreck with those that were shown on historic photographs that I obtained from the National Archives.

Victory Bond Cruise of Six ex-German U-boats

After Germany capitulated, Great Britain demanded the surrender of the Kaiser's navy. The capital ships were moved to Scapa Flow. Most of the U-boats were moved to Harwich; a few were moved to Plymouth. The German crews were interned; some of them were repatriated in 1919, but some were not repatriated until 1920.

During the winter of 1918-1919, the British government decided on the eventual disposition of approximately 180 surrendered U-boats. The majority was scuttled. A few were taken by Allied nations as part of war reparations.

The United States Navy requested six U-boats for exhibition to the American public in support of the Victory Bond Campaign (also called the Victory Bond Drive, the Victory Loan Campaign, the Victory Loan Drive, the Liberty Bond Campaign, the Liberty Bond Drive, the Liberty Loan Campaign, and the Liberty Loan Drive). This campaign or drive was implemented to encourage American citizens to buy war bonds. The government was suffering severe financial deficit due to the cost of the war; it needed to refill its flagging coffers in order to pay off extraordinary debts. The sale of bonds was one way to accomplish this. The government hoped that by the time the bonds matured, the money would be available to repay the original investment plus interest.

These U-boats were to be displayed in American cities the way the *UC-5* had been displayed in 1916.

It was decided that the U.S. Navy would assume ownership of the *U-117*, *U-140*, *U-164*, *UB-88*, *UB-148*, and *UC-97*. The U.S. Navy dispatched half a dozen naval officers and a hundred enlisted men from the Submarine Base at New London, Connecticut. Another thirty or so were gathered from various bases around the British Isles. All the officers had previous submarine experience, as did about half of the enlisted personnel.

This fleet of American U-boats was pretentiously called the Ex-German Submarine Expeditionary Force.

The first hurdle to overcome for the men who were assigned to this Force, was how to operate a U-boat. Although all submarine hulls share a similar shape, German submarines differed in layout from American submarines. The difficulties of handling this fleet of unfamiliar submarines were best described by Lieutenant Commander Joseph Nielson, who was assigned to command the *UB-88*:

"The German submarine is, naturally, a distinctive type. True, all submarines are built upon the same general principles, in that they have ballast and trimming tanks, diving rudders, motors, engines, etc. Still the arrangements and installation of all this material may be such as to present to a person who has had experience operating one type, a vessel in which everything will appear entirely different. Our previous experience was to be sure, of great value to us, but on account of the design of the German submarine, it was necessary 'to learn' these boats in every particular. For example: it is a very simple matter to blow tanks on a U.S. Submarine – but the problem was, how to blow them on the *UB-88*. First it was necessary to learn the operation of the German type of compressor. Next to learn the air distribution system to the different parts of the ship, then the leads to the air flasks or accumulators, then the leads from the flasks to the manifolds and from the manifolds to the tanks. this would put air into the tanks but it was further necessary to learn the operation of the ballast Kingston and the ballast vents. Then if you had been successful in following out the leads and valves, the problem was solved. This appears, no doubt, simple, and under ordinary conditions it would be, but the German arrangement of piping has not that beautiful symmetry found in our boats and a pipe may wind in and out among its fellows in such a way as to present a veritable Chinese puzzle. Blue prints and drawings were luxuries we did not enjoy, for all these had been very carefully removed.

"The cleaning, repairing where necessary, tracing out fuel oil lines, lubricating oil leads, air lines, water lines, ventilating pipes, battery leads, lighting circuits, took up a great deal of time allotted before the moving parts could be tried. All the name plates, naturally, were in German. We found that the German phraseology used in engineering was not the same we had learned in school. The amount of work necessary was apparent and the conditions under which we worked can be imagined.

"The *UB-88* was in a filthy condition. Food had been left aboard

There are two description papers on the back of this National Archives photo. The first reads, "Following the Armistice most of the German warships were turned over to the Allies. This depicts some fo the German submarines turned over. They are lying in the harbor of Harwich, England." The second one reads, "With a tug and a dozen men, we proceeded upriver to take over our new command. There, as far as one could see, the broad surface of the estuary was covered with U-boats, some 160 of them. They were secured in bunches - or 'trots' as the British called them - six or eight to each mooring buoy. They were paint-stained and rust streaked from months of disuse and lack of care. It was a sight to break the heart of any good submariner." *Down to the Sea in Subs*, Lockwood.' This would be Charles A. Lockwood, who was in command of the UC-97 dur the latter part of its tour in the Great Lakes, who fought in World War 2, and who rose to the rank of Rear Admiral before retiring.

At this time in the evolution of military undersea craft, Prime Minister Winston Churchill explained the difference between Allied submarines and German U-boats: ""Enemy submarines are to be called U-Boats. The term submarine is to be reserved for Allied under water vessels. U-Boats are those dastardly villains who sink our ships, while submarines are those gallant and noble craft which sink theirs."

after she had surrendered. The remnants of the last meals had been thrown in the bilges. The stench from the galley was unbearable. Rust covered all the piping. The engines were one mass of corrosion. The torpedoes had been pulled from the tubes and thrown on the torpedo room deck. The air flasks and after-bodies were coated with rust and badly pitted. The storage battery was almost run down, not having had a charge for over four months. The bilges were full of oil and water. Many parts of the boat had been taken by souvenir hunters while she lay moored in Harwich. The eye-piece on the forward periscope had been broken off and the reflecting prism and lens removed. The stabilizer had been taken from the gyro compass, as had also the azimuth motor. The magnetic compass had disappeared. Out of the dozen cooking utensils on hand, only one would cook, the rest had been smashed or the coils burned out. There were no mess gear, mattresses or blankets. There were no spare parts for the engines. Parts of the radio set had been stolen and the rest smashed in with a hammer. The repeaters for the gyro compass now decorated the homes of the British as souvenirs of the war.

"So many parts of the equipment were out of commission that it was decided to find out first what would work, then go after the parts that would not. This system was followed out. Everything was tested and report made whether or not it was in running order. If not, what was wrong, and what was needed to fix it. In a very short time we had a good estimate on just what we had to do.

"To illustrate our method: The radio set, as stated, had been demolished. The motor generator was there and would work, but sending and receiving sets were almost completely wrecked. By rummaging through about a dozen of the submarines still remaining in the 'Trot' [a nickname for Harwich Harbor], which were going to be sold for junk, we collected enough material to complete a sending set. We were unable to find a detector, however, so that had to be purchased in London, and with parts of a receiving set 'stubbed out' from the U.S.S. *Chester*, the radio outfit was complete, but not efficient. Probably it was the lack of harmony, due to the combination of English, German and American parts. Who knows? It was impossible to improve on the set until the arrival of the U.S.S. *Bushnell*. She had on board six complete outfits. By the addition of a quench gap and an audion bulb to what we already had, the outfit from one of these sets was connected up and tested. Our reward was a set with a hundred miles radius, which was sufficient for our needs.

"I stated before that the magnetic compass had been removed. Search was made through all the German submarines lying in the 'Trot' and none could be found. A U.S. Naval Vessel donated one, but it had been lying idle for so long in one position without any liquid in the bowl that the magnets had lost practically all their directive force. There was not much hope in getting good results from this compass, but nevertheless it was installed, and after filling the bowl, an attempt was made

The text that accompanied this photograph from the National Archives reads, "These four interior photographs of a German U-boat were in with the block of prints of the surrendered U-boats that came to America. There is no identification as to which boat they were taken in. A few words from Lockwood's impression of the boats might be of interest here. 'Our first difficulty was that of language. Except for one very smart chief machinist's mate, none of us knew any German. This made it impossible for us to read printed or stenciled German directives. Hence, it took a lot of crawling around, tracing out air and water lines, and cautious testing of valves and switches to discover just how the *UC-97* worked. . . .As might have been expected from the inventors of the diesel, the German engines were splendid and reversible. But, curiously enough, it was with our neat little M.A.N. 4-cycle engines that we *UC-97* sailors had our greatest trouble. Evidently the German Navy was short on lubricating oil, hence for these coastal boats they did not bother to hook up the piston-cooling lines. There was no way in which we could supply the missing parts. Stern necessity compelled us to follow the old injunction, "Make do with what you've got.",' *Down to the Sea in Ships*, Lockwood."

at compensation on one heading. That night before turning in I looked at the compass and it showed the heading NNW 1/4' W, which was about correct on magnetic North. I looked at the compass the next morning with the ship headed in the opposite direction (having swung with the tide) and it still showed us headed NNW 1/4' W. A call was made on the Senior Submarine Officer at the British Submarine Base, and after a 'search' he supplied us with a compass which had been taken from one of the German submarines. This was installed but on account of the binnacle being placed inside the chariot bridge, its operation was slow and sluggish. A make-shift stand was then installed between the periscopes on the periscope sheer. A block of wood placed directly under the center of the compass and bored with several holes at right angles, served admirably as a compensating rack and in this 'rig' we placed our hopes. True the steering wheel was about ten feet from the compass, but I don't think we worried much about that at the time.

"The German (Anshutz) type of gyro compass was a source of mystery. The stabilizer had been removed as had also the azimuth motor. By again visiting several of the boats up the 'Trot,' an azimuth motor was found and connected up. Also on the same trip we were fortunate in getting three repeaters in good condition. A stabilizer, however, could not be found. There was no one aboard who knew the interior construction of this type of gyro and in consequence no one knew how to operate it. By tracing up the leads from the compass, we found the motor generator and the power leads from the switch boards. That much settled, we went after the compass and by a process of trial and error, it was finally started, and much to the surprise of everyone, it worked satisfactorily. A four degree easterly deviation was removed by balancing the rotors with sealing wax placed in the compass levels to compensate for the loss of alcohol from the levels, which had been broken. The compass is still running perfectly. It has never shown any tendency to 'get off' the Meridian even in the roughest weather.

"The drainage system was of course, a vital problem, although a simple one. Trouble was experienced with the after trimming line pump and it has never been in good condition. The adjusting pump, just abaft the central control room, was working and as it could be connected up to all the bilges through the manifolds, full confidence was placed in this pump. If it had broken down completely the novel situation of bailing out a submarine with buckets or the use of a handy-billy would have resulted. Nothing else could have been done.

"As the safety of the boat on the trip from England to the United States was a paramount factor, it was thought advisable to [dry-]dock

Yet another photograph of the interior of one of the surrendered German U-boats that is part of the block of prints that is described in a caption on a prior page, and is courtesy of the National Archives.

the boats at Harwich before sailing. The underwater hull and all tanks were minutely examined. New Kingston gaskets were installed where necessary. The trustworthiness of our late enemies was never mentioned, still I do not doubt that it was in everyone's mind during the period of preparation. However, let credit be given them where it can, for we found no tampering of any kind. The boat was in dock two days, during which time very little opportunity was had for any progressive preparation. After undocking, however, we again turned to.

"The engines were the most important part of the equipment to prepare for operation. I think that everyone who worked on the engines did so with the determination to make them run as well or even better than the Germans had done. It was this or admit that the German crew was the better of the two. Looking at it in that light, the determination to succeed in the preparation of them was to everyone a matter which touched the most delicate spot in the human make-up – Pride.

"In beginning to learn the engines and auxiliaries, we were in the dark, except for our general experience with Diesel engines and the intimate knowledge of a few types which are used in our own service. As all engines of this type operate upon the same principle it was chiefly necessary to locate the supply, the discharge, if any, and the power of delivery of the circulating water, the air, and the lubricating oil. In the case of the fuel oil, the tanks were first located, then the leads, to the gravity feed tanks, and then the valves and pumps controlling the delivery to the engines. At the same time the fuel compensating system was traced out. The lubricating oil system was followed out and tested in the same way as was also the cooling water. In order not to forget the thousand and one valves with their German names, shipping tags were placed on each valve and gage. On these were written the use of the valve and how to operate it. The explanation of this procedure is brief and to the point and one would judge that we were occupied probably one or two days in this work of tracing out lines and tagging them. But so complicated and intricate was the German system of piping and valve arrangement that the time consumed before we were ready to start the engines was fourteen working days. When everybody had been properly prepared for our first trials of the engines, they were jacked over by hand to insure that everything was clear. The engine clutches were then thrown in and they were turned over slowly with the motors. All looked well. A signal was given to the electrician at the switch board to 'speed her up.' Slowly the lubricating oil built up the required pressure and the discharge pipes into the sight box on the side of the engine showed abundant supply to the piston heads. The circulating water pressure started to climb and was soon up to the required mark on the

This is the fourth photograph in the series of interior scenes of the surrendered German U-boats, which is part of the block of prints that is described in the lengthy caption on a prior page. (Courtesy of the National Archives.) Note the complexity of the mechanisms that fill nearly every available space inside the U-boat.

gage. The spray air pressure was slow in building up, but finally arrived at the proper mark. The oil supply was then opened and the cylinder try-cocks closed, and as the engines had run under the care of the Germans who had built them and studied their operation, so they ran then. There was not a hitch, nor had anything been forgotten. That day we charged batteries for four hours without stopping the engines, in order to be assured there would be enough power in the battery to turn the engines over the next time they were needed.

"After the crew had demonstrated their ability to run the engines, all hands 'turned to' to provide the necessities of life and what few comforts we could gather. The subs up the 'Trot' were ransacked for cooking utensils. We found plenty; terribly dirty and rusty. These we took, and after cleaning them and forgetting the condition in which they were found, the food prepared in them tasted very good. Plates, knives, forks and spoons, and the thousand and one things needed in the preparation and serving of food were purchased in London. Blankets, mattresses, pillows, life belts, sheets, etc., etc., were obtained from the Naval Depot, London. The Red Cross, always on the job when needed, provided us with woolen goods, pajamas, underwear, candy, chocolate, cigarettes, etc.

"Fuel, lubricating oil, provisions and water were taken from the U.S.S. *Bushnell* and the *UB-88* was ready."

Those U-boats that were cannibalized for parts were the ones that were later scuttled.

The date of departure was set for April 3, 1919. All six U-boats were supposed to travel in convoy with the *Bushnell*, but circumstances warranted otherwise. Only four U-boats departed on schedule: the *U-117, UB-88, UB-148,* and *UC-97.*

At nearly the last minute, the *UC-97* experienced trouble with one of its engines. The crew set out in the dark to liberate some spare piston heads from a sister ship. They returned successfully from their raid, and commenced to replace the broken pistons, but knew that they could not complete repairs before the 6:30 a.m. departure. They used the electric motors for propulsion. The *UC-97* closed with the *Bushnell.* The tender let a stout hawser off her stern. The towline was secured to the forecastle. The *Bushnell* towed the U-boat until repairs could be completed.

At 8:15 a.m., the *UC-97* suffered another mechanical malfunction: the steering gear jammed. The submarine veered out of control. Quick-thinking men slipped off the towline and turned hard to port in order to avoid ramming the *UB-88.* After the jammed steering gear was repaired, the towline was re-secured (at 9:30 a.m.). Operations proceeded fairly smoothly after this auspicious beginning.

Nielson provided the best description of the Atlantic crossing. The convoy started in hazy atmosphere, mild seas, and gentle ground swells, with the *Bushnell* leading the flotilla at 11 knots. They passed the White Cliffs of Dover and the coast of France. For three days they

Sub tender USS *Bushnell* escorted some of the surrendered German U-boats across the Atlantic Ocean, at times taking *UC-97* in tow when engine problems slowed the boat. "Alas for our calculations and portents, after the first few days of westward progress at eight knots speed - all that the *UC-97's* engines could produce - we ran into nothing but trouble. Gales, mountainous seas, blinding rain, and even snow swept down on us. It was fortunate we had a tender with us, for we could always [see] her masts or top lights. *Down to the Sea in Subs*, Lockwood." (Printed on the reverse side of this photographic print from the National Archives.)

proceeded southward in good weather. They encountered a passing squall on the fourth day. Two U-boats effected minor engine repairs that delayed the flotilla. On the seventh day they reached the Azores, where they spent two days in Ponta Delgada Harbor on the island of San Miguel. The U-boats took on water and provisions, and did more engine repairs.

The flotilla departed from Ponta Delgada on April 12. After one day of calm seas the flotilla ran into a storm that was more than a passing squall. "The waves built up with the wind and the seas broke over the starboard bow. Spray came continually over the bridge. All the hatches except the one in the conning tower were battened down. The boat rolled and pitched badly. This made it necessary for those men in the boat (except the ones on watch) to turn in their bunks or else be thrown from one side of the boat to the other with the roll and pitch."

Bad air resulted from malfunctioning circulating fans. Everyone suffered. Soon a gale was blowing. The topside watch was constantly inundated by wind-whipped spray. The interior of the hull was "damp and cold." The fierce storm raged for days.

"On the eighth day out the fresh water was found to be contaminated by fuel oil, which rendered it undrinkable. The distilled water, which was intended to be used for watering the batteries, had to be taken for cooking and drinking."

It snowed on the ninth day, with the wind increasing to a heavy gale. Then there was rain and hail, "and the continuance of the howling wind accompanied by the rocking and pitching of the boat."

Some of the submarines got separated. On April 21, the *U-117* was so far ahead that it was out of sight of the *Bushnell*. At the same time, the *UC-97* had engine trouble again, and was proceeding on one engine while repairs were being made to the other one. The *Bushnell* reduced speed so as not to lose sight of the ugly duckling that was in trouble.

On April 25, the deck log of the *UC-97* noted that the *UB-88* and *UB-148* were not in sight.

The *U-117* broke off from the flotilla and proceeded to New York on its own. Then the *UB-88* left the flotilla to continue its cruise solo. The storm finally abated.

"Two destroyers which had come out from New York to meet us appeared on the horizon and were soon alongside. Moving picture machines were turned on us. The officers and crews lined the decks to take a look at the German submarines. They stayed with us for about an hour, then they hauled ahead and slowly disappeared, headed for New York."

The *UB-88* entered the Gulf Stream and milder weather. The boat ran out of distilled water and "had to go to the fuel oil. In order to keep the crew from drinking the oily water, black coffee was always ready to be served. This did very well but did not quench the thirst as much as was sometimes desired. It was better, however, than the discomforts of the nausea caused by oily water."

Calm weather enabled the men to open the hatches and air out the interior. The crew took frequent strolls along the deck "holding to the life lines. Everyone took a new lease on life, smiles shone on faces where before there had been looks of anxious waiting. Razors appeared and did their much needed duty."

They sighted the New Jersey coast on April 25. The *UB-88* docked at the Sandy Hook army wharf at 4:30 in the afternoon. Two hours later the *UB-148* showed up. The next morning the *Bushnell* and the *UC-97* put in their appearance. All proceeded to New York and up the North River to the navy yard, which they reached at 8:15 a.m. on April 27.

Nielson did not give the time of arrival of the *U-117*. Other records indicated that it touched land slightly ahead of the other three and proceeded straight to the Brooklyn Navy Yard, where it arrived before nightfall on April 25. Even then it was not the first U-boat to reach the eastern seaboard. Imagine the surprise of the men in the *Bushnell* flotilla when they learned that another U-boat had reached the Brooklyn Navy Yard a full six days before any of the other U-boats.

Back in England, it was found that the *U-164* was in such horrible condition that its deficiencies could not be rectified in time to take part in the Victory Bond Campaign. The *U-111* was selected as a replacement. The newly assigned U.S. Navy crew worked prodigiously to prepare the chosen substitute for the Atlantic crossing, but it was not ready to depart until April 7, by which time the *Bushnell* and her bevy were already on their way.

Lieutenant Commander Freeland Daubin was in command of the *U-111*. Because the *Bushnell* and company had a three-day head start on him, he decided not to follow the others southward to the Azores before turning west, but to cut directly across the Atlantic Ocean by way of the great circle route.

According to Navy records, "Fogs, gales, and heavy seas harassed the U-boat all the way across the ocean. On one occasion, she came near sinking when she began filling with water because of an open seacock. However, one of her crewmen crawled under her engines and into the slimy dark water to find and close the offending apparatus. In spite of adversity, *U-111* made her passage successfully and moored in New York on 19 April."

The *U-111* garnered front-page headlines. "The *U-111*, the first of the German submersibles to arrive in the United States steamed into the Brooklyn navy yard at 8 o'clock tonight [April 19] in command of an American crew of four officers and 31 men. As the U-boat passed quarantine on the way up the harbor, she broke out the American flag at her main mast. The imperial German emblem floated below. Harbor craft gave her a salute of three guns."

What happened to the *U-140* has been obscured over time by the paucity of information and differing recollections. Even the Naval His-

torical Center admits to contradictions in the records: "Accounts vary as to how the *U-140* actually made the voyage to the United States. One source indicates that she made the voyage under her own power with *Bushnell* (Submarine Tender No. 2) and four of the other five U-boats of the Ex-German Submarine Expeditionary Force. On the other hand, in his account, Vice Admiral Charles A. Lockwood, Jr. – who served in and later commanded *UC-97* – stated that *U-140* preceded *Bushnell* and the four U-boats which sailed with her by several days. He also maintained that she was towed to New York by a collier, but he failed to identify the ship. Be that as it may, *U-140* arrived in New York sometime during May 1919."

If the *U-140* departed before the other U-boats, why did it not arrive until after they did – especially if it had been towed by a collier?

Nielson's published account appears to add confusion: "Promptly at the hour set, the *UC-97* cast off from alongside and headed down the bay, quickly followed by the *UB-141*, the *UB-88* and the *U-117*. The U.S.S. *Bushnell* brought up the rear."

I think it is fair to say that *UB-141* was a typographical error that should have read *UB-148* – the way it was written later in the article and in the performance report that Nielson wrote for the Navy.

Nielson does not mention that the *U-140* accompanied them, nor does the deck log of the *UC-97* (the only log of the six U-boats that the National Archives possesses). Additionally, the deck log of the *Bushnell* confirms that only the four U-boats noted above were in her escort.

Christie's Auction House added more confusion. In 2006, it put up for auction an item that was described as "Deck Log Book ex-German Submarine *U 140*/Month of march 1919". The description of the item reads, "For the dates 31 March 1919 to 14 July 1919 and documenting the names of the American crew, and documenting the delivery of the vessel from Chatham, England to Portsmouth, N.H., USA. This deck log gives a very good account of day to day life in the U.S. Navy after World War I and the work that went into dissecting this ex-German U-boat. Including the arrest of one worker on-board, injuries and illnesses, and the maintenance of the submarine. . . . It is interesting to note that the accounts of how she made her trip from England to the United States vary and that this log book clears up the story that she was towed to the U.S. by the U.S.S. *Saucoma.*"

This would seem to put paid to the mystery except for one thing – there has never been a U.S. Navy vessel named *Saucoma*. The solution might rest in the log book itself, but the successful bidder has not seen fit to publish anything about it.

The Naval Historical Center appears to be wrong in other regards: "The submarine was opened for a time to public viewing at New York. No records have been found delineating *U-140's* subsequent service. At the end of the summer, she was laid up at the Philadelphia Navy Yard and remained there, partially dismantled, until the summer of 1921.

Yet elsewhere, the historical record shows that the *U-140* was docked at the Portsmouth Navy Yard on May 7, 1920. Archival photographs of the *U-140* are captioned with that place and date. Philadelphia is in Pennsylvania (south of New York), whereas Portsmouth is in New Hampshire (north of New York). Where the U-boat spent the previous thirteen months would thus appear to be another mystery.

I was able to resolve all these inconsistencies and misinformation in one fell swoop. After intensive research I found mention of a Navy tug named *Sonoma* in connection with the *U-140*. When I looked into the matter by accessing the *Sonoma's* deck log for the relevant period, I discovered that she towed the *U-140* from Chatham, England to the Portsmouth Navy Yard by way of the Azores.

Tug and tow departed Chatham on June 10, 1919. They reached Ponta Delgada on June 20. The *Sonoma* took on coal during the night, then departed the following day with the *U-140* in tow. The U-boat never operated under its own power, but was towed all the way across the Atlantic Ocean. Tug and tow entered the Piscataqua River on July 4, and moored that day at the Portsmouth Navy Yard in New Hampshire.

According to the caption of another archival photograph of the *U-140*, although it was docked at the Portsmouth Navy Yard on May 7, 1920, it was docked at the Philadelphia Navy Yard on July 19, 1920, presumably where it underwent extensive examination by naval engineers until 1921. It took no part in the Victory Bond Campaign.

People swarmed over the decks of the four U-boats at the Brooklyn Navy Yard: reporters, photographers, Red Cross representatives, Army Salvation people, and salespeople for the Fifth Victory Loan, which was about to be launched. Meanwhile, crewmembers were kept busy with maintenance and repairs.

After the initial fanfare, the five participating U-boats were each assigned to visit different ports. They made news and sold bonds wherever they went. Millions of people flocked to see them. A privileged few actually got to go on board: only those who wore a button that signified their purchase of a bond.

The *UB-148* visited Connecticut cities along the north shore of the Long Island Sound: Bridgeport, New Haven, and New London. At the submarine base in New London, the U-boat was "subjected to extensive tests and trials to evaluate" performance capability. Afterward it was laid up at the Philadelphia Navy Yard.

The *U-111* toured New England, with major stops at the Massachusetts port cities of New Bedford and Boston. It traveled as far north as Portland, Maine. By September, it was docked at the submarine base at New London to undergo testing along with the *UB-148*. Then it was laid up at the Philadelphia Navy Yard.

The *U-117* visited Baltimore, Maryland before proceeding to the Washington Navy Yard in Washington, DC. May 22 was VIP day. The people who were given a tour of the U-boat included Secretary of the Navy Josephus Daniels, Secretary of War Newton Baker, Army Chief of

Although the historical evidence claims that the *U-140* remained in Portsmouth during its tenure prior to scuttling, the caption on this National Archives photograph reads "Navy Yard Phila. July 19 1920" in the lower left corner.

UB-88 on tour. (Courtesy of the North Carolina Museum of History.)

Staff General Peyton March, and other dignitaries. Daniels went so far as to crank the elevating wheels of the deck gun. The *U-117* remained there for quite a while before shuffling off to the Philadelphia Navy Yard for inactive duty.

At the Philadelphia Navy Yard, the *UB-148*, *U-111*, and *U-117* were partially dismantled, in some cases extensively. The top of the pressure hull above the engine room was removed from the *U-117*. This provided easy access to the engines. Individual parts and assemblies were removed and photographed. The interiors were essentially stripped of their components so that those components could be measured and studied. The deck guns were removed. What remained were hulks that hardly resembled terrible machines of war.

So much machinery and so many components were removed from the U-boats that by the time they were scheduled for scuttling, in 1921, they were not seaworthy enough to be safely towed to sea without a great deal of patching.

Naval and marine engineers had a field day removing "such apparatus from these submarines as will be of value . . . for further service and for test purposes. There will then remain a quantity of material, under the cognizance of the Bureau of Steam Engineering, such as main engines, their auxiliaries, instruments and various other electrical appliances for which the Government has no use. Many commercial concerns interested or engaged in submarine construction are desirous of securing much of this surplus material for study and test for the purpose of improving the design and character of their own product."

All this extra material was given away free of charge. Ultimately, of course, it would benefit the U.S. government in future submarine development.

In order to make Americans feel good about the superiority of U.S. submarines, the press waxed long about the inadequacies of German U-boats. This catered to a smug public and may have sold newspapers, but it contradicted the facts. The Navy's initial findings indicated:

"(a) The Diesel engines of these submarines are superior to any other Diesel engines in any other submarine in commission in the world.

"(b) The periscopes are equal, if not superior, to any other periscope.

"(c) The radius of action of these boats, type for type, is greater than that obtained by other nations.

"(d) Their double hull method of construction is probably superior to other types of construction, so far as protection against depth bombs is concerned."

Lieutenant Commander Holbrook Gibson, Commander of Submarine Repair Division, did not want to file an official report because of the adverse effect this knowledge might have within the Navy bureau. Nonetheless, due to the studies on U-boat diesel engines, the engines of the U.S. submarines *S-10*, *S-11*, *S-12*, and *S-13*, were redesigned using U-boat engines as models.

In his memoirs, Admiral Charles Lockwood noted that U-boats could dive faster than their American counterparts. Also, "Since German optical glass was the best in the world, their periscopes were excellent. Their tops were 'penciled' down to 20 millimeters – slightly less than one inch – which made them extremely difficult for enemy lookouts to spot. Our own periscopes were three inches or more at the top and not infrequently flooded. In the gyroscopic compass, the ingenious Germans had installed a second gyro designed merely to keep the instrument on an even keel; hence no bumbling in a heavy seaway.

"As might have been expected from the inventors of the diesel, the German engines were splendid – and reversible."

The *UB-88* and *UC-97* took different routes in their service to their newly adopted country.

With the Coast Guard cutter *Tuscarora* acting as tender, the *UB-88* departed from the Brooklyn Navy Yard on May 5. Three days later they entered the Savannah River and proceeded upstream to the municipal dock in Savannah, Georgia. Nielson gave a good account of their reception:

"The mayor of the city had been notified several days ahead of our intended visit and had been requested to give all publicity to the event. The result of this publicity was evident. The office forces in the buildings along the waterfront, all left their books and crowded to the windows; the dock employees, negroes handling cotton, stevedores

The control room of the *UB-88*. (Courtesy of the Naval Photographic Center.)

unloading ships, ship builders, everyone, quit work and looked at us as we slowly moved up the river. Steamers, dredges and factories all gave the three blast salute. No sooner had we moored than thousands flocked to the dock to make a more complete examination of the vessel. Brows [gangplanks] were placed fore and aft. Police officers were stationed at each brow to maintain order and to keep the crowds in line. One member of the crew was placed in each compartment to explain the different parts of the vessel to the visitors and to prevent parts of the vessel being carried away as souvenirs. Visitors were allowed everywhere except in the vicinity of the switch boards. As a matter of safety to them and to the boat, this part of the submarine was roped off. As the people would pass into each compartment the man stationed therein would point out the objects of particular interest and explain their uses. He would also answer any questions which were given him. Then by calling attention to something interesting in the next compartment the crowds were kept moving. The system worked admirably. It was found by actual count that an average of five thousand people a day could be shown through the boat in this way. The visitors after leaving the forward torpedo room were shown into the chief petty officers' quarters, then the officers' room, then to the central operating room, the pump room, the after battery room, the engine room and then through the engine room hatch to the deck where if they so desired, they could climb into the conning tower and look through the periscope."

The next stops were in Florida: Jacksonville, Miami, and Key West. The *Tuscarora* had boiler trouble so she remained at the navy yard in Key West to effect repairs. A minesweeper accompanied the *UB-88* northward in the Gulf of Mexico to Tampa and Pensacola. "In some cases the waiting line was half a mile long, the people standing two and three abreast. The patience shown in the presence of an almost intolerable heat may be a judge of the popularity of the *UB-88* on this cruise."

Then came Mobile, Alabama, where the U-boat stayed for four days. The *Tuscarora* rejoined the U-boat and went with it to New Orleans, Louisiana. After exhibiting the U-boat to record crowds, the *UB-88* proceeded up the Mississippi River to Baton Rouge, Louisiana; thence to Natchez, Mississippi; thence to Vicksburg, Mississippi; thence to Lake Providence, Louisiana; thence to Greenville, Mississippi; thence to Helena, Arkansas; thence to Memphis, Tennessee.

In Memphis the water became so shallow that the U-boat scraped on the bottom. The scheduled visit to St. Louis, Missouri had to be canceled.

The *UB-88* departed from Memphis on June 26. On the return downstream it stopped again at Greenville before continuing to New Orleans, where it arrived on July 1.

Nielson: "On the trip down the river a decided knock developed in the port tail shaft. This was due to the after strut bearings being worn away by the sand and grit of the river. It was so bad by the time the vessel reached New Orleans that [dry-]docking was necessary. As the only dock in New Orleans, the floating dock, at the Navy Yard, was in use, it was necessary to wait two weeks before it became available. The *UB-88* went into dock there on July 14. Upon examination it was found necessary to renew both strut bearings. These jobs were completed on July 22 and the vessel was undocked the same day."

The *Tuscarora* was replaced by the minesweeper *Bittern*, fresh out of the construction yard on her first assignment. She stayed with the U-boat for the rest of its journey.

The next stops were the Texas cities of Galveston and Houston. Pomp and ceremony accompanied the presentation of a miniature bale of cotton that was to become the first cotton bale to be transported through the Panama Canal to Los Angeles, California. The Panama Canal had opened five years earlier.

The *UB-88* departed for the Canal Zone on July 30. Nielson: "Bad weather was experienced during the entire last half of the trip. From the indications of the barometer and the shifting of the wind we were on the outskirts of a West Indian storm. Two hundred miles out of Colon a lubricating pipe to number one cylinder, starboard engine carried away, putting that engine out of commission. It was impossible to repair this at sea. In order to save time a tow line was taken from the U.S.S. *Bittern* and on the following day we entered Colon harbor. The two vessels moored at the Submarine Base, Coco Solo. Repairs were made and stores taken aboard. Saturday and Sunday the boat was open for inspection by the people of Christobal and Colon. On August 12 we sailed through the Panama Canal for Balboa, arriving there the same day. We remained in Balboa for two days to give the canal, army and naval officials and civilian employees an opportunity to visit the submarine. We also had the pleasure of entertaining the ex-president of Peru, the vice-president of Panama and many Panamanian officials."

Heading north along the West Coast, the *UB-88* stopped at Corinto, Nicaragua, then at Acapulco, Mexico.

Once again there was trouble with the starboard engine. Salt water found its way into the lubricating oil and crystallized on the piston heads. To break down the engine, remove the salt, and rebuild the engine would have taken a month. Instead, the ingenious submariners experimented with alternative methods of dissolving the salt: gasoline, kerosene, alcohol, hot water, and steam. Steam worked the best. They connected a steam line to the pump and increased the steam pressure to 100 pounds per square inch. That solved the problem.

The *UB-88* stopped at Magdalena Bay, then Manzanillo, and arrived in San Diego on August 29. From there it went to the California cities of San Pedro, Santa Barbara, Monterey, San Francisco, and the Mare Island Navy Yard; thence to the Oregon cities of Astoria and Portland; thence to the Washington cities of Seattle, Tacoma, the Bremerton Navy Yard, and Bellingham.

A close-up photograph of the net cutter on the *UB-88*. (Courtesy of the Naval Photographic Center.)

The return south along the coast took the *UB-88* to San Francisco again, then on to San Pedro, where the U-boat was laid up. The date was November 7.

Nielson estimated that the *UB-88* had traveled more than 15,000 miles since its departure from England, and had been seen by more than 400,000 "enthusiastic visitors." The U-boat never submerged during its entire time in American hands.

The *UB-88* languished in San Pedro for more than a year. It was partially dismantled during 1920: undoubtedly disemboweled like a beached whale, with its parts cut out and distributed among naval engineers for study.

The *UC-97* was still under the command of Lieutenant Commander Holbrook Gibson, who had taken it across the Atlantic. Escorted by the *Bushnell*, the U-boat slipped out of the Brooklyn Navy Yard on May 7. Its destination was the Great Lakes. It had barely poked its nose out of New York Harbor when it paused to conduct an anniversary ceremony. According to a newspaper account:

"On her deck lay a wreath of laurel, woodbine and fern, bound with a broad purple ribbon bearing the words: 'In Memoriam *Lusitania*.' Near the mouth of the Ambrose Channel the submarine's motors stopped, and the boat lay partly awash in the choppy sea. The skipper issued a command and up went the Stars and Stripes, the church flag, and underneath these went the German ensign. Then a bugle sounded 'taps.' With the last note the wreath fell to the surface of the sea. Silent after her sister ship after her murderous deed of May 7, 1915, the *UC-97* stole away."

Lockwood noted, "We who rode in the diminutive minelayer *UC-97* ran into fresh-water problems. The larger, longer-range submarines had ingenious fresh-water distillers operated from the hot gases of the main engine exhausts. We had no such equipment, only a very modest-sized fresh-water tank and no bathing facilities whatever except two washbasins. To complete the sanitary arrangements, there was one toilet for the entire complement of twenty-seven persons."

On May 16, the *Bushnell* and the *UC-97* arrived in Halifax, Nova Scotia. Then occurred a changing of the guard, with the *Bushnell* returning to New York and the U.S. Navy tug *Iroquois* escorting the submarine up the St. Lawrence Seaway and the St. Lawrence River.

According to the Naval Historical Center, "That assignment required her to negotiate the locks of the Canadian-controlled St. Lawrence canal system. *UC-97's* refusal to break with traditional practice on board a man-of-war and fly the Union Jack at the fore caused trouble at each Canadian port of call along the way. However, her commanding officer, Lt. Comdr. Charles A. Lockwood, Jr. – who later rose to fame in World War II as Commander, Submarines, Pacific Fleet – stuck to his guns and was later vindicated by Canadian naval officers who applauded his pertinacious observance of time-honored naval tradition. Once she cleared the last locks and entered the Great Lakes, *UC-97* began a whirlwind series of visits to American ports, large and small, along the littoral of Lakes Ontario, Erie, Huron, and Michigan. Though scheduled to visit Lake Superior ports as well, the U-boat had to cut short its voyage because of wear on the engines."

Wear on the engines was an understatement. Nearly all the piston heads were either cracked or in bad condition. Breakdowns were common. Replacement parts were either unavailable or long delayed in delivery.

June 2 found the two-vessel entourage at Sackett's Harbor, New York, in Lake Ontario. On June 4 they ascended the Oswego River to Oswego, New York. Visitors poured over the submarine for two days.

Gibson left the *UC-97* for an assignment in the District of Columbia, and the command torch was passed to his executive officer, Charles Lockwood.

The next stop was Charlotte, New York. Then came Toronto, Ontario; Burlington, New York, Port Dalhousie, Ontario.

The *Iroquois* was replaced by, appropriately, a pair of submarine chasers: the *SC-411* and the *SC-419*.

The Union Jack issue continued to plague the *UC-97* whenever it docked in a Canadian City. Lockwood related one instance that had a humorous ending. As the U-boat entered the last of twenty-seven locks that comprised the Welland Canal, a voice rang out through a megaphone, "Why don't you fly the Union Jack? Very rude of you Yanks to use our canal and not fly our flag." Chief Machinist's Mate Schaeffer cupped his hands and called, "Brother, we ain't flown that flag since 1776 – hadn't you heard."

After passing through the Welland Canal and entering Lake Erie, the three American warships reached Buffalo, New York on June 13. The *UC-97* entertained visitors for the next three days.

On June 17, they moved to Dunkirk, New York, then departed for Erie, Pennsylvania, which they reached before the end of the day.

Breakdowns were a constant problem. Despite mechanical adversities, the *UC-97* made more than thirty ports of call. Some of them were on the Canadian side of the border. It required all of June, July, and most of August to visit all these cities and exhibit the U-boat to eager crowds. The ultimate destination was Chicago, Illinois, in Lake Michigan, which the U-boat reached on August 19. There it was laid up at the Navy pier and taken out of commission.

During the next year the U-boat was stripped of most of its machinery and brass and copper fittings.

For the *UC-97* – indeed, for all six ex-German U-boats – there was only more port of call that they were destined to make. The submarines sat idle for the next two years, while arrangements were being made for their ultimate disposition.

The conning tower of the *UC-97*. Charles Lockwood is standing to the right. (Courtesy of the Submarine Force Library and Museum.)

SPECIAL REPORT

The 1921 Billy Mitchell Sinkings of ex-German warships off the Virginia Capes

Billy Mitchell was as controversial a general as the U.S. Army ever produced. He saw only reason, and was forced during his entire career to combat unthinking conventions. Then, as today, there was plenty of irrationality to fight. Mitchell's big bone of contention was the impotence of naval power in light of a technological innovation advanced by the Great War: the airplane. He knew before anyone else that his high speed gnats in the sky could wreak havoc on ponderous, slow-moving warships plying the coastal waters. Although the war had produced a recognizable body of evidence to support his views, the Navy and its career officers, steeped in the traditions of the sea, did not want to hear it. Mitchell set out to prove it to them.

The way he chose to do this was by demonstration. The ships he wanted to sink by aerial bombardment were the eleven German warships taken over by the U.S. government as reparations. (All were commissioned into the U.S. Navy).

The six U-boats reached the United States in the spring of 1919. Five of them arrived with the submarine tender *Bushnell* (AS-2) in a temporary fleet designated as the Ex-German Submarine Expeditionary Force. These were the *U-117, U-140, UB-88, UB-148,* and *UC-97.* The sixth, the *U-111*, was a last minute substitution for the severely damaged *U-164*, and made the crossing on its own.

These U-boats led a wide and varied career, galloping along the coast and stopping in port cities where they were exhibited to the public as part of the Victory Bond Drive. With the U.S. treasury in great debt, the U-boats became advertisements that encouraged people to buy bonds for the much needed Liberty Loan. By the end of the summer the U-boats were withdrawn from public viewing and turned over to Naval engineers, who disemboweled them like beached whales in order to study their design and mechanical systems.

The battleship *Ostfriesland*, the cruiser *Frankfurt*, and the destroyers *G-102*, *S-132*, and *V-43*, arrived the following year. A Navy memorandum stated that "the condition of the destroyers was such that the Board considered it a waste of money and time to attempt to put them in condition for steaming home." The *Ostfriesland* crossed the Atlantic under her own steam, but the others were towed.

Mitchell fought long and hard to convince his superiors to afford him the opportunity to demonstrate the bomber's might. Eventually, against its

Billy Mitchell in his flying outfit, at left. (Courtesy of the National Archives.)

will, the Navy was forced to accede to Mitchell's demands. During June and July of 1921, most of the ex-German warships were towed to the Southern Drill Grounds for a two part exercise: some to be bombed by Mitchell's airplanes, others shelled by Naval warships. More important politically than the means of destruction was the actuality itself: according to conditions of the Armistice, all German naval vessels were to be either scrapped, or sunk irretrievably, by August 9, 1921. They could not be saved as relics.

Mitchell overcame quite a few problems in carrying out his aerial display, least of which was the availability of ships to sink. The First Provisional Air Brigade needed planes, practice, and bombs. Mitchell mustered every biplane the Army possessed. He personally led flights of bombers over the target ship *San Marcos* (ex-*Texas*) off Tangier Island in the Chesapeake Bay, making run after run until his men scored 94% hits. The biggest aerial bomb then in existance was a 1,000-pounder: suitable against a submarine, but not large enough to sink a battleship. Mitchell had specially made one-hundred-fifty 2,000-pounders and seventy-five 4,000-pounders.

The Navy did everything it could to stymy Mitchell's plans: it appealed directly to Washington that the general was a madman, that the country needed a stronger Navy and had no allocations for an air force, that planes could have no effect against thickly armored warships. When the Navy lost the battle to prevent Mitchell from gaining support for his bombing experiments, it tried to have the target ships placed so far offshore that the airplanes would be forced to operate at the extreme limit of their range: the fuel capacity of early biplanes was not great. When Mitchell got wind of this final subversion, he put pressure in the proper places and got the ships moved closer to shore. The orders finally issued called for all ships to be sunk "beyond the fifty fathom curve."

By this time so much machinery had been removed from the U-boats that they were no longer seaworthy enough to be towed to sea to be sunk. Naval and marine engineers had a field day removing "such apparatus from these submarines as will be of value ... for further service and for test purposes. There will then remain a quantity of material, under the cognizance of the Bureau of Steam Engineering, such as main engines, their anxiliaries, instruments and various other electrical appliances for which the Government has no use. Many commercial concerns interested or engaged in submarine construction are desirous of securing much of this surplus material for study and test for the purpose of improving the design and character of their own product." All this extra material was given away free of charge. Ultimately, of course, it would benefit the U.S. government in future submarine development.

The Navy's initial findings indicated that:

"(a) The Diesel engines of these submarines are superior to any other Diesel engines in any other submarines in commission in the world.

(b) The periscopes are equal, if not superior, to any other periscope.

(c) The radius of action of these boats, type for type, is greater than that obtained by other nations.

(d) Their double hull method of construction is probably superior to other types of construction, so far as protection against depth bombs is concerned."

Lieutenant Commander Holbrook Gibson, Commander of Submarine Repair Division, did not want to make a report because of the adverse effect this knowledge might have within the Navy bureau. Although information released to the news media stated otherwise, due to the studies on U-boat diesel engines, the engines of the U.S. submarines *S-10*, *S-11*, *S-12*, and *S-13*, were redesigned using U-boat engines as models.

In the U-boats, hull plates were replaced and riveted, pipes and openings blanked where fittings had been removed, and loose material adrift in the superstructure was secured. Despite these precautions, the *U-111* sank in the Chesapeake Bay and missed the trials; she was not raised until the following year. During the U-boat exercises no U.S. submarines were allowed at sea between Long Island and Charleston, SC. Five motion picture concerns were granted permission to accompany the Naval observers in order to photograph the historic events.

Of the three U-boats to be sunk off the Virginia Capes, Mitchell's planes were allowed to bomb only one: the *U-117*. The *U-140* and the *UB-148* were sunk by gunfire. The *UB-88* was shelled by the *Wickes* (DD-75) off San Pedro, California, and sunk in 300 feet of water. The *UC-97* was shelled and sunk by the gunboat *Wilmette* in Lake Michigan, in a depth of some 200 feet.

The aerial bombardment of the *U-117* was a glowing success. Mitchell had six flights of planes lined up to make bombing runs. The three planes of the first flight straddled the anchored U-boat, and a direct hit from the second flight sent her to the bottom. The Navy made excuses: the *U-117* was a small unarmored submarine; the effect on a large capital ship would not be so dramatic.

Meanwhile, destroyers shelled the remaining two U-boats with much less proficiency. The *Dickerson* fired thirty-nine shots at the *U-140*, of which nineteen scored hits; it took an hour and twenty-four minutes for the U-boat to sink. The *Sicard* scored twenty hits out of forty shots fired at the *UB-148*; it took eleven minutes to register the first hit, and another twenty-nine minutes for the U-boat to sink. A Navy memorandum stated succinctly, "valuable data secured from destruction." If Naval officers had been open-minded, they would have realized that the most valuable datum was that aerial bombardment was more effective than shelling.

Exercises were also carried out on the decommissioned battleship USS *Iowa* (BB-4), renamed *Coast Battleship No. 4*. She became the first radio controlled target ship used in fleet exercises. Secretary of the Navy Josephus Daniels outlined the purpose of the "experiments to determine the present value of aircraft operating from shore bases against naval vessels unattended by aircraft."

His memorandum stated, "Actual bombing tests from the aircraft so concentrated, using dummy bombs of standard size, form, and weight against the U.S.S. IOWA, steaming at her highest practicable speed and maneuvering under radio control. These tests are for the purpose of determining the accuracy with which bombs can be dropped over the sea." This was carried out on June 29.

Navy flying boats were sent out first to search for the *Iowa*, then to bomb her. It took them four hours to locate the target. Then, they dropped eighty bombs and scored only two hits. Navy pundits augured that Mitchell would do no better with his army planes on the ex-German warships. But they did not reckon on Mitchell's constant drilling with his men and planes.

The *Iowa* was not sunk at this time, but served in her capacity as a radio controlled target until March 23, 1923, when she was sunk in Panama Bay by a salvo of 14-inch shells.

By July 13, Mitchell was ready to attack the *G-102* with eighteen SE-5 pursuit planes armed with machine guns and light bombs, De Havillands armed with 100-pound bombs, and Martin bombers armed with 600-pounders. The SE-5s raked the decks with pinpoint precision and riddled the hull from bow to stern. Mitchell waved off the De Havillands and brought in the heavy bombers straightaway. Twenty minutes later, the *G-102* lay at the bottom of the ocean. The Navy was still unimpressed, making excuses for the destroyer's quick demise.

Two days later, rather than letting Mitchell repeat his performance, Navy ships sank the other two German destroyers by gunfire: the *S-132* by the *Delaware* (BB-28) and the *Herbert* (DD-160), the *V-43* by the *Florida* (BB-30).

Next on Mitchell's agenda was the *Frankfurt*. The Navy insisted, with good reason for a change, that he work over the cruiser with small bombs first, then work his way up to the larger ones. Flight after flight of planes dropped 100-pounders all morning, with long intervals between attacks during which observers from the *Shawmut* (CM-4) boarded the derelict and inspected damage. In this instance the Navy was very methodical in studying the results, finding that even 250- and 300-pound bombs were unable to penetrate the upper decks. Goats and others animals, stationed topside to simulate human crews, were found dead and macerated, but the ship itself was intact.

Navy inspectors, smugly deciding that aerial bombs alone could never sink the cruiser, ordered the *North Dakota* (BB-29) to prepare a time bomb. Then came Mitchell's Armageddon with the 600-pounders dropped by heavy Martin bombers. They rained down so fast and furiously that the *Frankfurt* was immediately shrouded in spray; tons of sea water fell upon her decks. Crews on the observation ships ran for cover as steel fragments ripped across the water for more than a mile. Before the attack could be called off, so observers could board and make damage assessments, the *Frankfurt* slipped beneath the waves. Photographic planes recorded with a vengence the events of July 18.

The ultimate test was yet to come. The *Ostfriesland* was protected by twelve inches of armor plate; she had four skins for protection against mines and torpedoes; she had so many watertight compartments that it was thought impossible to sink her. At the Battle of Jutland she survived a mine explosion and eighteen hits from large shells. She was a floating fortress of arms and armament.

On July 20, the *Henderson* was packed to the gunwales with over three hundred distinguished guests; in addition to some fifty reporters, there were eight Senators, twelve Congressmen, three Cabinet members (the Secretaries of War, Navy, and Agriculture), and foreign observers from England, France, Spain, Portugal, Brazil, and Japan. The *Pennsylvania* was loaded with admirals, generals, and other high ranking military officers.

The day dawned miserably, with thirty knot winds whipping the sea to a froth. Mitchell and his flyboys sat idly at Langley Field, awaiting the call to strike. When nothing was heard by 1300, Mitchell jumped in his Osprey and flew out to sea. The Navy wanted to call off the attack because of weather. Mitchell insisted that the bombing raid be carried out as planned, stating that his planes could fly under those conditions if Navy men could observe under them. He went so far as to order his planes into the air without Naval approval.

The Navy was struck by his impudence, but allowed the attack to proceed. Unfortunately, the 250-pound bombs did little damage to the *Ostfriesland's* steel hide. Mitchell's planes landed in a blinding rain storm as reporters were racing for shore aboard the *Leary* (DD-158) to report that the battleship was "absolutely intact and undamaged." Many seasick VIPs also returned to shore, convinced that the planes had lost the day.

Mitchell was not to be dissuaded from his convictions. The next morning found him readying his planes with blockbuster 2,000-pound bombs. At first he was allowed to drop only the 1,000-pounders. Two scored direct hits, and the Navy called off the rest of the attack so they could send observers aboard. They found the *Ostfriesland* so badly torn up that they were unable to go below the third deck; they peered through gaping bomb holes at the water seeping in below.

Then came the big bombs. One by one seven Martin and Handley Page bombers made their drops, aiming for near misses, and timing it so that each tremendous waterspout settled before the next plane came in for its attack. The concussion of exploding bombs was so severe that observation ships pounded when the shock wave reached them; planes at an altitude of 3,000 feet rocked violently. Thousands of tons of water descended upon the *Ostfriesland's* decks.

The third bomb scored a direct hit on the forecastle; it tore out a frightful hole in the steel hull, and created a raging fire. Another near miss lifted the battleship visibly out of the water. Bomb number five fell near the stern. The *Ostfriesland* began settling aft. When the sixth bomb hit, the after two turrets were already underwater. The battleship's bow nosed upward, the ship rolled over onto her port side, and disappeared from view. A Handley Page delivered the final stroke by dropping the last bomb on the huge vortex of escaping air.

Although Mitchell was ecstatic, the Navy refused to accept the implications of his success. It continued to put down the general's allegations that a strong and separate air force would change the tide of future warfare. Mitchell refused to back down from his position. Soon, he was railroaded out of the country on foreign assignments intended to lose him in red tape and obscurity. Eventually, as he kept up his verbal attack against Naval ignorance, using the press as his sounding board, he was brought up on charges of subversion, and court-martialed.

Mitchell was in nationwide headlines for months. His trial was the news of the decade. In a kangaroo military court the general was eventually "suspended from rank, command and duty with the forfeiture of all pay and allowances for five years."

This censure did not prevent Mitchell's predictions from coming true. As early as 1923 he forecast the buildup of Japanese air power, and outlined in detail how they would attack Pearl Harbor and Clark Field. It happened exactly as stated in his report—a report pigeonholed by military minds not prepared to face American vulnerability.

Obviously, the Honorable G. Katsuda, member of the House of Peers of Tokyo, was more impressed by the aerial display of might than his American counterparts. He was on board the *Shawmut* as an observer when the *Ostfriesland* was successfully bombed. Ironically, when the Japanese bombed Hawaii's battleship row two decades later, the *Shawmut* (renamed *Oglala*) was sunk at her berth during the attack.

Perhaps July 21, 1921 was the real day of infamy.

Final Dispositions of Virginia Capes Sinkings

June 22, 1921: *U-117* (Submarine): aerial bombardment
June 22, 1921: *U-140* (Submarine): *Dickerson*
June 22, 1921: *UB-148* (Submarine): *Sicard*
July 13, 1921: *G-102* (Destroyer): aerial bombardment
July 15, 1921: *S-132* (Destroyer): *Delaware* and *Herbert*
July 15, 1921: *V-43* (Destroyer): *Florida*
July 18, 1921: *Frankfurt* (Cruiser): aerial bombardment
July 21, 1921: *Ostfriesland* (Battleship): aerial bombardment
August 31, 1922: *U-111* (Submarine): *Falcon*

Other Dispositions

January 3, 1921: *UB-88* (Submarine): *Wickes* (off San Pedro, California)
June 7, 1921: *UC-97* (Submarine): *Wilmette* (in Lake Michigan)

Locations of Virginia Capes Sinkings

Ken Clayton's exhaustive study of the anchorage locations of the ex-German warships led to positively identifying the positions of the *Frankfurt* and *Ostfriesland* (q.v.), and to other "hang" positions that are exact but which cannot definitely be ascribed to a particular vessel other than distinguishing between submarine and destroyer.

G-102 (?)	26823.4	41640.4
Destroyer	26824.0	41717.0
Destroyer	26818.0	41718.0
Submarine	26873.5	41569.5
Submarine	26874.0	41573.0

The following are close but appear slightly too deep to be the submarines (50-55 fathoms), although they should be checked out.

Unknown	26833.0	41547.0
Unknown	26839.2	41548.2
Unknown	26838.6	41552.8

Courtesy of the North Carolina Division of Archives and History, Raleigh.

U-117

Commissioned (German Navy): March 28, 1918 Sunk: June 22, 1921
Commissioned (U.S. Navy): March, 1919 Depth: Unknown
Displacement tonnage: 1,164 surfaced; 1,512 submerged
Type of vessel: Submarine Dimensions: 267′ × 24′ × 13′
Builder: Aktiengessellschaft Vulcan, Hamburg, Germany
Armament: One 5.9-inch gun, one 3.4-inch gun, four torpedo tubes, two mine tubes with 42 mines. Power: Diesel
Cause of sinking: Aerial bombardment
Location: Southern Drill Grounds

Although the *U-117* had time for only one war patrol before the signing of the Armistice, it was highly successful. Under the command of Kapitanleutnant Otto Droscher, it left Kiel on July 11 and headed straight for America. It made its presence known on August 10, when it encountered a fleet of fishing boats off the Massachusetts coast and ripped into their flanks with guns blazing. In very short order nine fishing boats were sent to the bottom by either gun fire, or boarding and bombing. The crews were allowed to escape in their dories.

Two days later, the *U-117* torpedoed the Norwegian freighter *Sommerstad* south of Long Island. In addition to carrying out its mine-laying operations, the *U-117* made surface and submerged attacks on merchant shipping. During the next three weeks she accounted for the *Dorothy B. Barrett, Madrugada, Mirlo, Nordhav, Rush, Bergsdalen, Elsie Porter,* and *Potentate.*

The *U-117* had been home for two weeks before its mines were discovered. On October 4, off Barnegat Light, New Jersey, the Mallory Line steamer *San Saba* was the first to strike one of the infernal machines; she went down in fifteen minutes. Only six of her thirty-seven man crew survived. On October 27, the Cuban freighter *Chaparra* struck another mine in the same field. Although the ship went down in five minutes, all but six of the crew got away in two lifeboats; the twenty-three survivors rowed to shore at Beach Haven and North Beach (across the inlet from Barnegat.)

193

The final sinking of the war occurred only two days before the signing of the Armistice, when the USS *Saetia*, a military cargo ship, blundered into the Fenwick Island minefield off the Maryland coast. Eighty-five men suffered great travails as they were plunged into the sea, or climbed aboard rafts and lifeboats that rocked violently in rough seas. Fortunately, all survived.

The *U-117* remained active upon return to Germany. At the cessation of hostilities it was surrendered to Allied forces at Harwich, England. On April 3, on its own power, it once again crossed the Atlantic, this time under a U.S. Navy crew.

After doing a stint for the Victory Loan campaign, it was towed to a spot sixty miles off Cape Charles. On June 22, 1921, it was sunk as a result of a direct hit from a single 165-pound bomb dropped from a Navy F-5-L seaplane.

Below left: An F-5-L seaplane. Below right: A bomb devastates the *U-117*. (Both courtesy of the National Archives.) Bottom: The *U-117* and the *U-140* moored to a buoy in the Southern Drill Grounds. (Courtesy of the Smithsonian Institution.)

194

U-140

Commissioned (German Navy): March 28, 1918 Sunk: June 22, 1921
Commissioned (U.S. Navy): March, 1919 Depth: 265 feet
Displacement tonnage: 1,930 surfaced; 2,483 submerged
Type of vessel: Submarine Dimensions: 311′ × 29′ × 17′
Builder: Germania, Kiel, Germany Power: Diesel
Armament: Two 5.9-inch guns, two 3.4-inch guns, six torpedo tubes
Cause of sinking: Gunfire from USS *Dickerson* (DD-157)
Location: 26874.1 41574.5

The *U-140* was the third of six U-boats that attacked the American east coast during the summer of 1918. Korvettenkapitan Waldemar Kophamel never brought his submarine close to shore; the seven vessels he sank all went down in deep water. The huge guns carried by the *U-140* enabled him to sink by shell fire the 10,289 ton steamship *O.B. Jennings* off the Virginia coast, as well as the 7,523 ton British steamer *Diomed*. He torpedoed the 7,029 ton Japanese steamship *Tokuyama Maru*. On his nearest incursion, Kophamel brought the *U-140* to within one hundred fifty yards of the *Diamond Shoals* lightship and, after allowing her crew to escape, blasted her apart. On the same day he also sank the *Merak* by gunfire. See *Shipwrecks of North Carolina: from the Diamond Shoals North* for accounts of both sinkings.

Although it sank only seven ships compared to thirty-six sunk by the *U-117*, the *U-140's* total of 30,594 tons sent to the bottom lagged by only 3,000 tons the record of the *U-117*.

After that single patrol, the *U-140* sat out the remainder of the war. It was turned over to the British at Harwich, England, on February 23, 1919. After a tour of duty for the Victory Loan campaign, it was partially dismantled at the Philadelphia Navy Yard. It was sunk by gunfire from the *Dickerson*, with nineteen hits out of thirty-nine shorts fired.

On June 6, 1992, while searching for wrecks aboard the *Miss Lindsey* (Captain Mike Hillier), we dropped anchor on a "hang" number that turned out to be a submarine we believe to be the *U-140*. During this initial exploration the group of thirteen divers surveyed the stern section from the conning tower aft. The wreck sits upright with the pressure hull intact. The outer skin and the upper catwalk are gone, leaving the after hatch coaming protruding some three feet above the pressure hull. The hatch was closed. The conning tower fairweather is missing; about eight feet of the enclosed conning tower rises above the hull. The propeller shafts are buried. Considerable breakdown at the extreme stern obscures the after torpedo tube doors.

The divers who participated in this historic event were, in alphabetical order, Ken Clayton, Ric Culliton, Peter Feuerle, Alexander Hamilton, Jon Hulburt, Barb Lander, Bart Malone, John Moyer, Gene Peterson, Brad Sheard, Brian Skerry, Harvey Storck, and the author.

These pictures of the *U-140* were taken on May 7, 1920 at the Portsmouth Navy Yard, New Hampshire. Below is the after ammunition trunk. Both views on the right show the deck forward of the conning tower. (All courtesy of the National Archives.)

Courtesy of the Submarine Force Library and Museum

UB-148

Never commissioned in the German Navy — Sunk: June 22, 1921
Commissioned (U.S. Navy): March, 1919 — Depth: Unknown
Displacement tonnage: 523 surfaced; 653 submerged
Type of vessel: Submarine — Dimensions: 182′ × 19′ × 12′
Builder: Aktiengessellschaft Weser, Bremen, Germany
Armament: One 3.4-inch gun, five torpedo tubes — Power: Diesel
Cause of sinking: Gunfire from the USS *Sicard* (DD-346)
Location: Southern Drill Grounds

The *UB-148* was a small coastal submarine which was launched on August 7, 1918, but not completed before the Armistice. At first interned at Karlskrona, Sweden, it was later surrendered to the British at Harwich, England. On April 3, 1919, it left for America to participate in the Victory Bond drive. After a short cruise along the coastal ports north and south of New York City, it underwent extensive trials and performance tests. Then it was laid up at the Philadelphia Navy Yard and partially dismantled. It later joined in the gunnery tests along with the other ex-German warships.

The *UB-148* docked next to the U.S. sub *L-8*. (Both courtesy of the Submarine Force Library and Museum.)

Target Cruises
of the Billy Mitchell Wrecks

In accordance with the terms of the Treaty of Versailles, all captured or surrendered German navy vessels that were in the hands of the Allies had to be scrapped or destroyed by July 1, 1921. They could not be saved as relics. An addendum extended the deadline for capital ships by one month. A vessel could be considered destroyed if it were scuttled irretrievably in water that was too deep to permit its salvage.

On January 3, 1921, the U.S. minesweeper *Pokomoke* towed the *UB-88* out to sea off San Pedro, California. On board was a moving picture crew whose purpose was to record an historic event for posterity. The *Pokomoke* came to a halt about eight miles south-southeast of the Los Angeles breakwater light.

Accompanying the pair was the U.S. destroyer *Wickes*. In command of the *Wickes* was Commander William Halsey, who became a famous admiral in World War Two, known affectionately as Bull Halsey. The *Wickes* had an observation party on board.

At 4:08 in the afternoon, the *Wickes* opened fire with three of its deck guns. For two minutes the guns fired furiously at the *UB-88*. The U-boat sank by the bow four minutes after the *Wickes* ceased fire.

That wrapped up operations for the day. The *Wickes* left the site at 4:20, passed the breakwater light at 4:40, and was back in port by 4:55. It was a short day's work that was done with very little fanfare.

There seems to be a great deal of confusion about the date of the sinking of the *UB-88*. Most secondary sources give the date as March 1, 1921. I suspect that this is because someone at the Naval Historical

Center made a mistake during the compilation of the *Dictionary of American Naval Fighting Ships*, in which the entry for the *UB-88* notes, "On 1 March 1921, she took her final plunge when *Wickes* (DD-75) sank her with gunfire." DANF is the main source that is used by casual researchers. DANF is not without errors, some of the gross.

The deck logs of the *Wickes* and *Pokomoke* both confirm the sinking date as January 3. So how did this error come about? My guess is that one of the compilers wrote the date numerically as 1/3/21, and that someone else transposed the month and day, and wrote 3/1/21. Thus the DANF entry is incorrect by posing the date two months early.

According to the California Department of Transportation, District 10, Jeffrey R. Delsescaux, the *UB-88* was discovered by Gary Fabian in July 2003. "Fabian used publicly available multibeam sonar data from the United States Geological Survey's (USGS) Pacific Seafloor Mapping project to identify the wreck. Later, local divers used the same methodology to relocate the wreck themselves around 2010, and freely distributed the wreck coordinates. The wreck has since become a popular diving attraction for technical divers."

The *UB-88* lies in 190 feet of water in San Pedro Bay.

On June 7, 1921, the USS *Hawk* towed the *UC-97* to a point in Lake Michigan some 25 miles outside of Chicago, Illinois. Again there was very little fanfare.

Designated to sink the U-boat by gunfire was the USS *Wilmette*. Before its present incarnation, the *Wilmette* was the passenger steamer *Eastland*. The *Eastland* was notoriously known as one of the worst steamship disasters ever to occur in the Great Lakes. Because of inherent instability problems, she rolled over at her dock when she had a full load of passengers on board, resulting in the drowning deaths of more than eight hundred people. The wreck was raised, stripped of its superstructure, then reconstructed in the form of a gunboat.

After taking on a party of observers, the *Wilmette* weighed anchor at 8:17 in the morning. She soon caught up with the *Hawk* and the *UC-97*. All stopped at the predetermined site at 10:20 a.m. They idled for more than an hour, until sub chaser *SC-412* came alongside the *Wilmette* and transferred the Naval District commandant and another party of observers.

At 11:45, the *Wilmette* opened fire with her 4-inch battery. During the course of the next five minutes she fired eighteen rounds at the *UC-97*. The U-boat sank by the head barely ten minutes after the *Wilmette* ceased fire. The sub chaser departed the site at 12:10 p.m. The job was done.

According to a newspaper account, "At Waukegan, Zion City and other north-shore cities the roar of the naval guns caused considerable excitement. Police headquarters and north-shore newspaper offices were swamped with inquiries about the 'earthquake.' "

As retired U.S. Navy officer James Wise wrote, "This was the first

UC-97 on display during the Victory Bond Drive. (From the Willard Jaques collection.)

time that a U.S. naval gun had fired an explosive shell on any of the Great Lakes since Commodore Oliver Hazard Perry defeated the British on Lake Erie in September 1813."

According to a dubious article from the Naval History and Heritage Command, an outfit called A and T Recovery located the site of the *UC-97* in 1992. I heard rumors of this so-called discovery throughout thirty years of diving in the Great Lakes, but was never able to trace the rumor to its primary source. All I could ever find was someone who knew someone who knew someone who knew someone who had found the wreck.

Many of the divers I met during my Great Lakes excursions thought that the wreck had been found, but no one knew who found it or where.

On one dive trip to the Great Lakes, I met a man who said that he had confirmation of the discovery of the *UC-97* in the form of underwater video footage that not only showed the wreck, but showed the U-boat's number on the conning tower. He offered to show the videotape to me. I went to his house one night in order to view the screening on his television set.

He inserted the videotape into the player and tapped the "play" button. The image focused on a vertical section of what presumably was an iron hull. Flood lights illuminated orange rust which, because the water was fresh instead of saline, was not encrusted with marine organisms. (This was prior to the zebra mussel incursion.) The camera panned from left to right in water that was clear with average visibility.

Particulate matter was slight.

When the videotape ended, I said something like, "Where was *UC-97* painted on the conning tower?"

In fact, I never saw the conning tower. All I saw was a horizontal pan of a rusty hull. To show the conning tower, the camera would have had to rise above the deck. A pan of a hull could have been taken on any one of a thousand shipwrecks in Lake Michigan.

He shook his head. "I swear I saw it before."

This was the kind of person who sees what he wants to see, such as believers in flying saucers and the Loch Ness monster.

He had no explanation for why he saw the letters and numbers before but didn't see them now. The power of suggestion works only when the suggester is present.

Did A and T Recovery truly find the *UC-97*, or was the outfit perpetrating a hoax? Words are cheap but do not locate shipwrecks.

In science, the results of laboratory experiments are considered to be invalid unless they can be repeated by other laboratories. Because A and T Recovery did not release the coordinates of the wreck site, no one else can verify or confirm that the *UC-97* was ever really found.

The story of the scuttling of the other four ex-German U-boats is deeply intertwined with that of U.S. Army General Billy Mitchell. After the U.S. entered the Great War, Mitchell was sent to France to organize American flying units to fight against Germany. He was a pilot who led his men by example. At war's end, he returned to the U.S. with a firm conviction that the future of warfare lay in aerial combat.

Mitchell became as controversial a figure as the Army ever produced. He saw only reason, and during his entire military career he was forced to combat unthinking conventions. Then, as today, there was plenty of irrationality to fight.

Hawk **towing the** ***UC-97*** **to the scuttling site.**
(From the author's collection.)

The cachet on this envelope was designed to commemorate the first day of issue of the Billy Mitchell stamp. The image depicts biplanes after they released their bombs on the battleship *Ostfriesland*.

His big bone of contention was the impotence of naval power in light of a technological innovation that had been advanced by the Great War: the airplane. He realized before anyone else that these high-speed gnats in the sky could wreak havoc on ponderous, slow-moving warships that plied the coastal waters.

Although the war had produced a recognizable body of evidence to support his view, the Navy and its career officers, who were steeped in the traditions of the sea, disagreed with him. Mitchell set out to prove to the Navy that capital ships were not invulnerable to attack from the air. The way he decided to do this was by demonstration.

The vessels that he wanted to sink by aerial bombardment were the German warships that had been taken over by the U.S. government in order to study their design features. In addition to the six U-boats that comprised the Ex-German Submarine Expeditionary Force, there were three destroyers (*G-102*, *S-132*, and *V-43*), the cruiser *Frankfurt*, and the battleship *Ostfriesland* – eleven vessels in all.

They were all slated for destruction by the terms of the Treaty of Versailles. The Navy completed its performance testing. Except for the *UB-88* and *UC-97*, the rest were laid up in Navy bases along the eastern seaboard.

The nine warships were assembled at Lynnhaven Roads, which lay at the mouth of the Chesapeake Bay. The Navy prepared to scuttle them in deep water off the coast of Virginia – somewhere "beyond the fifty fathom curve." Fifty fathoms equals three hundred feet.

The Navy wanted to use the ex-German warships for gunnery practice. Mitchell wanted to bomb them from the air.

Mitchell had to jump a number of bureaucratic hurdles in order to convince politicians and his military superiors to grant authority for him to proceed with his endeavor. The Navy did everything it could to stymy his plans: it appealed directly to Washington that the general was a madman, that the country needed a stronger Navy and had no allocations for an air force, that planes could have no effect against thickly armored warships.

When the Navy lost the battle to prevent Mitchell from gaining support for his bombing experiments, it tried to have the target ships placed so far offshore that the airplanes would be forced to operate at the extreme limit of their range. The fuel capacity of early biplanes was not great. When Mitchell got wind of this final subversion, he put pressure in the proper places and got the ships moved closer to shore.

Mitchell also had some logistical problems to consider. The First Provisional Air Brigade needed planes, practice, and bombs. Mitchell mustered every biplane that the Army possessed. He personally led flights of bombers over the target ship *San Marcos*: the battleship *Texas* under a new incarnation. The target ship lay off Tangier Island in the Chesapeake Bay. His flyboys made run after run until they scored 94% hits on the target.

The biggest aerial bomb then in existence was a 1,000-pounder: suitable against a submarine, but not large enough to sink a battleship. Mitchell had larger bombs made to his specifications: one hundred fifty

My very good friend and dive buddy Bart Malone found this framed color print in an antique shop. Knowing of my connection with the German battleship *Ostfriesland*, he bought it for me. It hangs on a wall in my study.

2,000-pounders and seventy-five 4,000-pounders.

The U-boats were in deplorable condition. So much machinery had been removed from them, and so many hull fittings had been tampered with, that they were no longer seaworthy enough to be towed to sea without fear of sinking along the way. They had to be patched for their final cruise. Damaged or missing hull plates were replaced and riveted. Openings had to be blanked where pipes had been removed from the hull. Loose material in the superstructure had to be secured. The barely floating hulks were towed to Lynnhaven Roads and placed on moorings that swung with changes in the tide.

The U-boat tests were scheduled for June 22. The hulks were towed off the Virginia capes and anchored. The tests proved hardly a thing.

The destroyer *Dickerson* sank the *U-140* by gunfire, with nineteen hits out of thirty-nine shots fired. It took an hour and twenty-four minutes for the U-boat to sink.

The destroyer *Sicard* sank the *UB-148* by scoring twenty hits out of forty shots. It took eleven minutes to register the first hit, and another twenty-nine minutes for the U-boat to sink.

The only U-boat that Mitchell was allowed to bomb was the *U-117*. He had six flights of planes lined up to make bombing runs. The three planes of the first flight straddled the anchored U-boat with bombs. On the second flight, a direct hit from a single 165-pound bomb that was dropped from a Navy F-5-L seaplane sent the U-boat to the bottom like a rock. The remaining four flights did not have the opportunity to enter the demonstration.

A Navy memorandum stated succinctly, "Valuable data secured from destruction." If Naval officers had been open-minded, they would have realized that the most valuable datum was that aerial bombardment was more effective than shelling.

This is the end of the story as far as U-boats are concerned: a small bang that was hardly more than a whimper. Yet in order for the reader to fully comprehend events that occurred in 1941, and later in 1990, I need to put the U-boat story in grand historical perspective.

The Navy made the excuse that the *U-117* was a small, unarmored submarine. The effect of bombs on a large capital ship would not be as dramatic.

Exercises were conducted on the decommissioned battleship *Iowa* (renamed *Coast Battleship No. 4*). She became the first radio controlled target ship to be used in fleet exercises. Secretary of the Navy Josephus Daniels outlined the purpose of the "experiments to determine the present value of aircraft operating from shore bases against naval vessels unattended by aircraft."

His memorandum stated, "Actual bombing tests from the aircraft so concentrated, using dummy bombs of standard size, form, and weight against the U.S.S. IOWA, steaming at her highest practicable speed and maneuvering under radio control. These tests are for the purpose of determining the accuracy with which bombs can be dropped over the sea." This was carried out on June 29.

Navy flying boats were dispatched first to search for the *Iowa*, then to bomb her. It took them four hours to locate the target. Then, they dropped eighty bombs and scored only two hits. Navy pundits argued that Mitchell could do no better with his army planes on the ex-German warships. But they did not reckon with Mitchell's constant drilling with his men and planes.

The *Iowa* was not sunk at this time, but served in her capacity as a radio controlled target until March 23, 1923, when she was scuttled in Panama Bay by a salvo of 14-inch shells.

Direct hit on the *G-102*.
(Courtesy of the National Archives.)

By July 13, Mitchell was ready to attack the *G-102* with eighteen SE-5 pursuit planes that were armed with machine guns and light bombs, De Havillands that were armed with 100-pound bombs, and Martin bombers that were armed with 600-pounders. The SE-5's raked the decks with pinpoint precision and riddled the hull from bow to stern. Mitchell waved off the De Havillands and brought in the heavy bombers straightaway. Twenty minutes later, the *G-102* lay at the bottom of the ocean. The Navy was still unimpressed, making excuses for the destroyer's quick demise.

Two days later, rather than let Mitchell repeat his performance, Navy ships sank the other two German destroyers by gunfire: the *S-132* by the battleship *Delaware* and destroyer *Herbert*, the *V-43* by the battleship *Florida*.

Next on Mitchell's agenda was the *Frankfurt*. The Navy insisted, with good reason for a change, that he work over the cruiser with small bombs first, then work his way up to the larger bombs. Flight after flight of planes dropped 100-pounders all morning, with long intervals between attacks, during which observers from the minelayer *Shawmut* boarded the derelict and inspected the damage that the bombs had inflicted. In this instance the Navy was very methodical in studying the results, finding that even 250- and 300-pound bombs were unable to penetrate the upper decks. Goats and other animals, stationed topside to simulate human crews, were found dead and macerated, but the ship itself was intact.

Navy inspectors, smugly inferring that aerial bombs alone could never sink the cruiser, ordered the battleship *North Dakota* to prepare

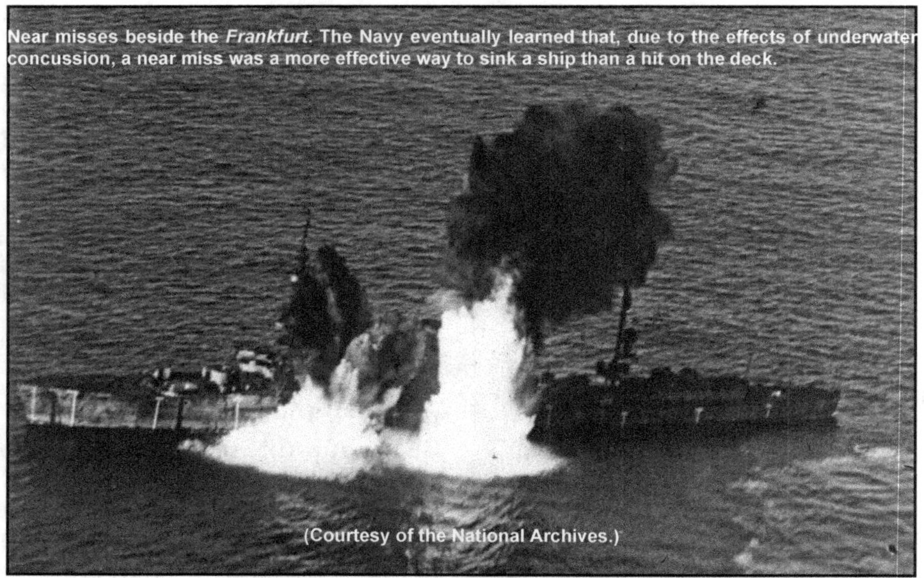
Near misses beside the *Frankfurt*. The Navy eventually learned that, due to the effects of underwater concussion, a near miss was a more effective way to sink a ship than a hit on the deck.

(Courtesy of the National Archives.)

a time bomb. Then came Mitchell's Armageddon with the 600-pounders dropped by heavy Martin bombers. Bombs rained down so fast and furiously that the *Frankfurt* was immediately shrouded in spray. Tons of seawater fell upon the decks. Crews on the observation vessels ran for cover as steel fragments ripped across the water for more than a mile. Before the attack could be called off, so that observers could board the cruiser and make damage assessments, the *Frankfurt* slipped beneath the waves. Photographic planes recorded with a vengeance the events of July 18.

The ultimate test was yet to come. The *Ostfriesland* was protected by twelve inches of armor plate. The hull had four skins for protection against mines and torpedoes. The battleship had so many watertight compartments that naval experts thought that the vessel was impossible to sink. At the Battle of Jutland, the *Ostfriesland* survived a mine explosion and eighteen hits from large shells. It was a floating fortress of arms and armament.

On July 20, the troop transport *Henderson* was packed to the gunwales with more than three hundred distinguished guests. In addition to some fifty reporters, there were eight Senators, twelve Congressmen, three Cabinet members (the Secretaries of War, Navy, and Agriculture), and foreign observers from England, France, Spain, Portugal, Brazil, and Japan.

The battleship *Pennsylvania* was loaded with admirals, generals, and other high-ranking military officers. More than a score of other U.S. warships surrounded the *Ostfriesland*.

The day dawned miserably, with thirty-knot winds whipping the sea to froth. Mitchell and his flyboys sat idly at Langley Field, awaiting the call to strike. When nothing was heard by one o'clock in the afternoon, Mitchell jumped into his Osprey and flew out to sea. The Navy wanted to call off the attack because of weather. Mitchell insisted that the bombing raid be carried out as planned, stating that his planes could fly under those conditions if Navy men could observe under them. He went so far as to order his planes into the air without Navy approval.

The Navy was struck by his impudence, but allowed the attack to proceed. The 250-pound bombs did little damage to the *Ostfriesland's* steel hide. Mitchell's planes landed in a blinding rain storm as reporters were racing for shore aboard the destroyer *Leary*, to report that the German battleship was "absolutely intact and undamaged." Many seasick VIP's also returned to shore, convinced that the planes had lost the day.

Mitchell was not to be dissuaded from his convictions. The next morning found him preparing his planes with blockbuster 2,000-pound bombs. At first he was permitted to drop only the 1,000-pounders. Two scored direct hits, and the Navy called off the rest of the attack so they could send observers on board. They found the *Ostfriesland* so badly torn up that they were unable to go below the third deck. They peered through gaping bomb holes at the water that was flooding into the hull below.

Then came the big bombs. One by one, seven Martin and Handley Page bombers made their drops, aiming for near misses, and timing them so that each tremendous waterspout settled before the next plane approached for its attack. The concussion of exploding bombs was so

Shortly prior to sinking, *Ostfriesland* takes a devasting hit from aerial bombardment. (From the author's collection.)

severe that observation vessels pounded when the shock wave reached them. Planes at an altitude of 3,000 feet rocked violently. Thousands of tons of water descended upon the *Ostfriesland's* decks.

The third bomb scored a direct hit on the forecastle. It tore out a frightful hole in the steel hull, and ignited a raging fire. Another near miss lifted the battleship visibly out of the water. Bomb number five fell near the stern. The *Ostfriesland* began to settle aft. By the time the sixth bomb struck, the two after turrets were already under water. The battleship's bow nosed upward, the ship rolled over onto its port side, and it disappeared from view. A Handley Page delivered the final stroke by dropping the last bomb on the huge vortex of escaping air.

Although Mitchell was ecstatic, the Navy refused to accept the implications of his success. The Navy Department continued to ridicule the general's allegations that a strong and separate air force would change the tide of future warfare. Mitchell refused to back down from his position. Soon, he was railroaded out of the country on foreign assignments that were intended to lose him in red tape and obscurity. Eventually, as he kept up his verbal attacks against Navy ignorance, using the press as his sounding board, he was brought up on charges of subversion, and was court-martialed.

This censure did not prevent Mitchell's predictions from coming true. As early as 1923, he forecast the buildup of Japanese air power, and outlined in detail how they would attack Pearl Harbor and Clark Field. It happened exactly as he stated in his report – a report that was pigeonholed by military minds that were not prepared to face America's vulnerability.

In the event, the Honorable G. Katsuda, member of the House of Peers of Tokyo, was more impressed by the aerial display of might than his American counterparts. He was on board the *Shawmut* as an observer when the *Ostfriesland* was successfully bombed into submission. Ironically, when the Japanese bombed Hawaii's battleship row two decades later, the *Shawmut* (renamed *Oglala*) was sunk at her berth during the attack.

Perhaps July 21, 1921 was the real day of infamy.

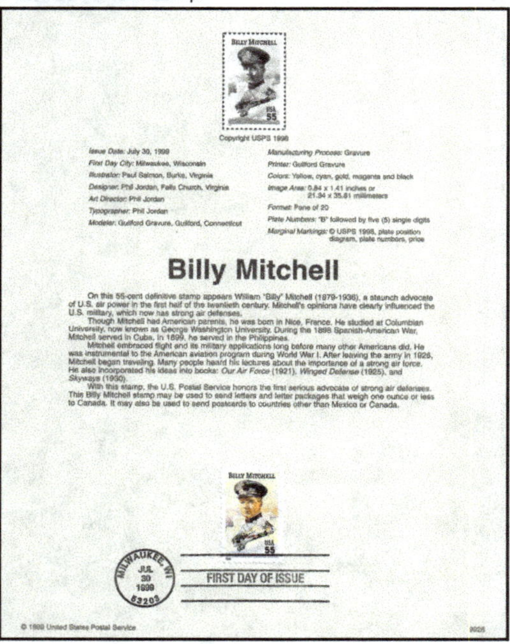

BILLY MITCHELL
USA 55

Copyright USPS 1998

Issue Date: July 30, 1999
First Day City: Milwaukee, Wisconsin
Illustrator: Paul Salmon, Burke, Virginia
Designer: Phil Jordan, Falls Church, Virginia
Art Director: Phil Jordan
Typographer: Phil Jordan
Modeler: Guilford Gravure, Guilford, Connecticut

Manufacturing Process: Gravure
Printer: Guilford Gravure
Colors: Yellow, cyan, gold, magenta and black
Image Area: 0.84 x 1.41 inches or 21.34 x 35.81 millimeters
Format: Pane of 20
Plate Numbers: "B" followed by five (5) single digits
Marginal Markings: © USPS 1998, plate position diagram, plate numbers, price

Billy Mitchell

On this 55-cent definitive stamp appears William "Billy" Mitchell (1879-1936), a staunch advocate of U.S. air power in the first half of the twentieth century. Mitchell's opinions have clearly influenced the U.S. military, which now has strong air defenses.

Though Mitchell had American parents, he was born in Nice, France. He studied at Columbian University, now known as George Washington University. During the 1898 Spanish-American War, Mitchell served in Cuba. In 1899, he served in the Philippines.

Mitchell embraced flight and its military applications long before many other Americans did. He was instrumental to the American aviation program during World War I. After leaving the army in 1926, Mitchell began traveling. Many people heard his lectures about the importance of a strong air force. He also incorporated his ideas into books: *Our Air Force* (1921), *Winged Defense* (1925), and *Skyways* (1930).

With this stamp, the U.S. Postal Service honors the first serious advocate of strong air defenses. This Billy Mitchell stamp may be used to send letters and letter packages that weigh one ounce or less to Canada. It may also be used to send postcards to countries other than Mexico or Canada.

BILLY MITCHELL
USA 55

MILWAUKEE, WI JUL 30 1999 53203

FIRST DAY OF ISSUE

© 1999 United States Postal Service

9926

United States Postal Service information sheet which provided specifications about the Billy Mitchel first day cover, including a franked 55-cent stamp.

Underwater Cruises

As the saying goes, "out of sight, out of mind." So it was for the ex-German U-boats and capital ships that were scuttled beyond reach. By the end of the twentieth century, only a few people in the world remembered them, and fewer cared.

I was one of the few who both remembered and cared.

In the mid-1970's, I started to research what I eventually came to call the Billy Mitchell Wrecks: those one-time warships of the German fleet that were scuttled off the Virginia Capes. My original interest was inspired by my quest to discover shipwrecks whose locations were unknown.

At the National Archives in Washington, DC, I examined records that related to the bombing and gunnery tests of 1921. When I saw that the ex-German warships were slated for scuttling "beyond the fifty fathom curve," in order to make them inaccessible to salvors, I quit my research on the Billy Mitchell Wrecks because a working scuba dive to those depths was considered impractical, if not impossible.

Some fifteen years later, in 1989, I resumed my research on the Billy Mitchell Wrecks. My renewed interest came about because I was engaged in a massive project to write a series of books about shipwrecks along the American eastern seaboard: the Popular Dive Guide Series. I reviewed my notes, returned to the National Archives, and accessed the same records again, but this time with the idea of simply obtaining primary documentation to enable me to write an historical account for inclusion in *Shipwrecks of Virginia.*

Wilkes-Barre

I spent a week in compiling information. During that week I was scheduled to give a slide presentation to a local dive club called Capitol Divers. At the meeting I met Ken Clayton – a fairly new and overeager diver I had met several months before while diving on the U.S. cruiser *Wilkes-Barre,* which had been scuttled in 1972 in an underwater demolition test off Key West, Florida. The wreck lay at a depth of 250 feet.

Now comes one of those coincidences which, had it been written in a novel, would have appeared contrived. Clayton showed me a book that contained a picture of the *Ostfriesland*, and asked me if I knew anything about it. I told him that I had been researching the battleship that very day. I gave him the bad news about the depth: 380 feet. He accepted it with equanimity.

The story of my friendship with Clayton, and ground-breaking dives that we did together over the next seven years, I have already related in exquisite detail in my two-volume history of wreck-diving, *The Lusitania Controversies*. The bulk of that saga lies beyond the scope of the present volume.

Suffice it to say that we embarked on a dedicated program to discover the locations of the Billy Mitchell Wrecks. By noting the positions of the numerous observation vessels, and triangulating the bearings and distances of each to the various German warships, we developed a picture of the relationship of each vessel to every other vessel.

Both Ken and I curried the favor of fishing boat captains who shared with us their "hang" logs. A hang log is a list of coordinates – loran or GPS numbers – on which commercial trawling vessels have "hung" or snagged their nets. In order to avoid losing additional expensive gear, trawler captains maintained records of nasty places to shun. Most hangs were boulders, ledges, or geological outcrops. About one in ten was a shipwreck.

Pete Manchee, the author, and Ken Clayton hold an Explorer's Club flag over the *Ostfriesland*.

I bought a bathymetric chart of the area. Clayton correlated from hang numbers with wreck symbols that were depicted on the chart. There were differences to be sure – in 1921, the observation vessels used sextant, chronometer, and mathematics to calculate their positions; in the 1980's they used time delays from transmission stations to an onboard receiving unit: a system called long range navigation, or loran. There was no satellite global positioning system in those days.

Then we chartered a boat to visit the sites and confirm their existence by means of a depth sounder. All this work enabled us to pinpoint the final resting place of the *Ostfriesland* – our primary goal. As noted above, the wreck lay at a depth of 380 feet.

Pete Manchee came onboard as part of the dive team. In order to consummate a dive on the wreck, we had to invent an entire new order of diving: a quantum leap beyond what was recognized as recreational diving.

Instead of breathing air, which is composed primarily of oxygen and nitrogen, we breathed what is known as mixed gas: either heliox (oxygen and helium) or trimix (oxygen, helium, and nitrogen). This was necessary because, at extreme depth, nitrogen was narcotic and oxygen was toxic. We also had to plan on decompressing for two hours or more in the open ocean while breathing various blends of nitrox from bottles, and oxygen that was fed to us through hoses from a storage bottle on the surface support vessel: the dive boat *Miss Lindsey*, Captain Mike Hillier.

The triumvirate made the first *Ostfriesland* dive in 1990. In subsequent years, Ken and I made more dives on the *Ostfriesland*. We also located and dived on the destroyers *G-102*, *S-132*, *V-43*,and the deepest one of all: the cruiser *Frankfurt* (at 420 feet).

More relevant to the topic of this book are the three U-boats that were scuttled in the vicinity of the capital ships. We discovered all three. I can still feel the elation of that first find.

At a depth of 200 feet, the cerulean blue water below showed no sign of ending. I raised my eyebrows at my dive buddy, Ken Clayton. He shrugged. The current was strong and my arms were feeling the strain of the pull down the anchor line. We paused for a moment to rest. It wasn't good to get out of breath at depth, so we paced ourselves accordingly. We didn't know how deep we had to go in order to touch the wreck that we hoped lay silently on the bottom.

At 210 feet the water continued greenish blue and featureless. At 220 it was the same. At 230 I began to see a dim ghostly outline ahead. At 240 the shadowy shape took on definite form. It was the hull of a sunken vessel.

Ambient light visibility was nearly 50 feet, the result of Gulf Stream intrusion which sometimes brushed the offshore waters of Virginia. At 250 feet I could see the hull distinctly. The side facing us rose vertically to an upper edge that curved back to form the deck; the plating was remarkably well preserved. The thinly encrusted metal cast little reflected light, and the overall dull gray was mottled with splotches of lighter shades in a nearly monochromatic design.

What I could see of the wreck so far looked like a submarine.

My exhilaration turned to anxiety when I saw that the grapnel had not hooked the hull, but the sand!

The grapnel had dragged over the top of the wreck, had fallen to the white sandy bottom on the down-current side, and had snagged with a single tine on something that lay completely buried. With a vise-like grip on the anchor line in case the grapnel suddenly came free, I dropped to the sand to examine the stability of the hook.

Although only one tine had caught, it was gripped firmly on the edge of a thick steel plate that lay at a distance of only one foot from the place where the hull met the sand. No matter how hard I twisted and yanked, I could not move the grapnel – and the boat above to which it was secured – against the force of the current. I raised my eyebrows at Ken, who hovered above me and oversaw my actions. He nodded.

I let got of the line. Instinctively I felt behind my tanks for my decompression reel, just in case. My depth gauge registered 266 feet. We kicked upward and alighted upon the deck about fifteen feet above the seabed. What looked like the end extended to our left, so we went right.

In just a minute or two we reached an upright structure that was distinctly discernible as a conning tower. And not the conning tower of an American sub, but of a German U-boat. And not just any U-boat, but a World War *One* U-boat.

Specifically, the *U-140*. The date was June 6, 1992.

On that dive, Ken Clayton and I became the first divers in the world to touch a World War One U-boat that was sunk in American waters.

The next U-boat on our discovery agenda was the *UB-148*. According to our historical documentation, the wreck lay close to the *U-140* in about the same depth. We had a promising location. On a subsequent trip, we anchored into the *U-140* for the benefit of those who had not dived it before. The rest of us saved our dive time and breathing gas for the "new" U-boat – hoping, of course, that we could find it.

Chris Stone went down alone. When he returned, Mike Hillier, captain of the *Miss Lindsey*, couldn't get the grapnel out. Stone bounced down and cut the tines free from the net in which they were snagged. Afterward, listening to Stone describing the wreck, Ken and I had a creepy feeling that either he had been narked the whole time despite breathing mixed gas, or . . .

. . . Hillier had gotten the numbers swapped and took us to the wrong coordinates. Thus Chris Stone made not only the first dive on the *UB-148*, but the first *two* dives!

With the wreck rehooked, Ken and I dived separately and alone, although our paths crossed several times on the bottom and on the anchor line: characteristic wreck-diving buddy technique. Thirty feet of ambient light graced the seabed, but I cringed when I saw how tenuous the grapnel was set: it had caught in a twisted knot of netting that was stretched taught to a point some fifteen feet off a break in the hull. The strain of the boat prevented me from budging the grapnel to reset it in metal. When I examined the net closely, I saw with relief that within the mass of rope and twine a thick steel cable lay embedded. I went exploring.

This net was the "hang" that was the origin of the loran numbers.

About twenty feet of the bow had been blown off, exposing two long bronze torpedo tubes, one of which lay almost completely free and appeared to be easily recoverable. The ten-foot gap between the forward compartment and the pressure hull was knitted together by the net in

U-140
© Ben Roberts

UB-148
© Ben Roberts

which the grapnel was hooked. The wreck sat upright, and the shell of the conning tower rose about eight feet above the rusting deck. Twenty feet off the port side of the conning tower, a string of buoys floated a net off the bottom like a thick lace curtain suspended from rods. Abaft the conning tower on top of the hull gaped a hole the size of a double door. I should have been able to peer into the engine room, but the interior was filled with sand and silt to within three feet of the rim.

The depth to the bottom was 274 feet. The date was August 17, 1992.

The *U-140* and the *UB-148* had been shelled by surface vessels, but the *U-117* had been sunk by aerial bombardment from Billy Mitchell's planes. The reason we looked for the *U-117* last, despite its importance to our overall quest to dive on those particular vessels that were sunk by Mitchell's bombers, was a function of progressive depth exploration. Naval records indicated that the *U-117* went down where the water was 300 feet deep. We were working our way down, so to speak.

From historical accounts we chose the most probable location and correlated it with the hang numbers that we had in the area. The following year, after hours of searching with negative result, we resignedly moved off site to check out another set of numbers nearby, but only 230 feet deep. Any unexplored wreck could be interesting.

This time we got lucky and found the numbers right on target. Ken Clayton and Peter Hess went down first. Just as they began their ascent, the grapnel pulled out and the boat went adrift, so the rest of us had to wait out their decompression before entertaining the possibility of a dive. When they finally surfaced, we were as astonished as they were to learn that the wreck was that of a submarine!

I knew of three U.S. submarines that had been scuttled off the Virginia coast, and concluded that we must have stumbled onto one of them. When we rehooked the wreck, the anchor chain fell across the edge of the conning tower, which I studied in detail without observing anything that provided clues to the sub's identity. Dark, dismal conditions prevailed on the bottom, almost like a night dive. I did not stray far.

The date of this discovery was August 12, 1993.

For two years I agonized over which sub it could be. Then we returned on a day in 1995 when visibility exceeded fifty feet ambient. I took a grand tour from end to end. It was immediately obvious how the wreck's location became known: the towing yokes of two trawler rigs, expensive shipwreck locator devices, were firmly implanted in the starboard hull.

Not until I examined the stern carefully and compared my sketch with historical photos did I recognize the distinctive slope as the after deck above the minelaying tubes. It was the *U-117* all along, misplaced by both leagues and fathoms.

Through those tubes once slid the mines that sank the *Chaparra*

U-117
© Ben Roberts

and the *San Saba* off the New Jersey coast, and the *Saetia* off Maryland. Through one of the tubes in the bow sped the torpedo that sank the *Sommerstad* off Long Island's southern shore, and the *Mirlo* off North Carolina, in that long ago year when war raged over the world.

There is more to behold and explore on these wrecks than I have seen for myself or described. They are three of a kind, if you will, together comprising a rare insight into Germany's first undersea and most effective killing machine, and the precursor of deadly events to come a generation later.

To dive on the Kaiser's U-boats is to touch the heart of history.

Billy Mitchell. (From the author's collection.)

Courtesy of Submarine Force Library and Museum.

Courtesy of the National Archives.

U-111

Commissioned (German Navy): December 30, 1917 Sunk: August 31, 1922
Commissioned (U.S. Navy): March, 1919 Depth: 1,600 feet
Displacement tonnage: 798 surfaced; 996 submerged
Type of vessel: Submarine Dimensions: 235′ × 20′ × 11′
Builder: Germania, Kiel, Germany Power: Diesel
Armament: One 4.1-inch gun, one 3.4-inch gun, six torpedo tubes
Cause of sinking: Charges placed by USS *Falcon*
Location: 37-45-15 N 74-07-45 W

The *U-111* made three war patrols during her short career, all around the British Isles. It sank one ship on the first cruise, two on the second, and none on the third. At the cessation of hostilities it was turned over to the British at Harwick, England.

When the Allies allocated six U-boats to assist the United States in the Victory Bond drive, one of them, the *U-164*, was found to be in such a deplorable state that it could not be put into condition for the Atlantic crossing. For that reason the *U-111* was picked as a replacement. By the time it was placed in commission, the Ex-German Submarine Expeditionary Force had already left for the States.

The *U-111* left four days later, on April 7, taking the great circle route. It had a rough passage, encountering gales and mountainous seas. An open sea-cock nearly sank the U-boat, but an enterprising American seaman crawled through the bilge water under one of the engines and managed to close the valve. The *U-111* arrived at New York on April 19.

Its participation in the Victory Bond campaign consisted of a tour of New England port communities. Afterward, it underwent a series of

The *U-111* soon after arrival in the States (left) and soon after salvage (right). (Both courtesy of the National Archives.)

performance tests. Then it was laid up at the Portsmouth Navy Yard until orders were received to prepare it for explosives tests off the Virginia Capes.

On June 13, 1921, the minesweeper *Quail* (AM-15) began towing the *U-111* to Lynnhaven Roads, Virginia. On the 14th the U-boat appeared to be down by the head by about four feet; it remained in that attitude for the rest of the voyage. Upon their arrival at their destination on June 16, the *U-111* was secured to a mooring buoy and an inspection was made. A Navy memorandum stated:

"On opening the hatch of the forward torpedo compartment this compartment was found full of water. The wrecking pump of the tug was able to lower the level of this water until it could be seen that a considerable stream was coming from one of the torpedo tubes. The rear door of this tube had been removed at the Navy Yard as had also the hand-wheel for operating the bow door. An inspection of the compartment next astern of the torpedo room showed that there was practically no water in this compartment. No anxiety was felt for the vessel and it was intended to improvise a tube shutter on the morning of 17 June. The *Quail* remained alongside the vessel all night pumping intermittently."

The pump was disconnected in the morning as the *Quail* proceeded to shove off for other duty. The *U-111* began settling quickly. "An inspection of the compartment next astern showed that some of the wooden plugs in the inner hull of the vessel had come out and that this compartment was also flooding. Two plugs, one of them about six inches in diameter were seen to blow out about this time."

The *Quail* rerigged the towing lines and tried to beach the U-boat. On the way to shore, the *U-111's* bow grounded in five fathoms. Slowly, the stern sank, until the U-boat rested on the bottom with three feet of water over the conning tower.

No salvage equipment was available in the 5th Naval District. It was therefore suggested that the USS *Falcon* (ASR-2) be assigned to raise the U-boat. At that time the *Falcon* was conducting salvage operations on the USS *S-5* (SS-110). On September 3, more than a year after the *S-5* went down, and after 477 dives had been made by Navy hardhat divers, she was given up as lost. (See *Shipwrecks of Delaware and Maryland*, by this author.)

A gas buoy with a red flashing light was placed on the wreck of the *U-111*, at 36-56-20 N and 76-04-00 W. Six mooring buoys were set. The *Falcon* arrived on October 1. After a month and a half of hard work the *Falcon* was called off for other duty. She wintered in New York, where she underwent a refit. It was not until June 1922 that she returned to the site of the *U-111*. Divers eventually managed to seal the open torpedo tube, and replace the wooden plugs that had popped out of the inner hull. On July 29 the *Falcon* pumped air into the U-boat's compartments, but succeeded in raising only the stern.

On August 4, she towed two pontoons to the wreck site. After much hard work in attaching the pontoons to the sunken hull, the *U-111* was finally raised and towed to drydock at the Norfolk Navy Yard on August 14. There the U-boat was repaired well enough so it could be towed to sea for scuttling.

The *Falcon* was bound for the Portsmouth Navy Yard on August 30, with the *U-111* lashed to her starboard side. Aboard the salvage vessel was Mr. H.D. Blaunet, of the Pathe Moving Picture Company, who was assigned the task of photographing the sinking. Once in the open sea the U-boat was dropped behind on a hundred fathoms of wire. The following day, when the *Falcon* reached the prearranged site, a charge was detonated in the forward battery room, blowing a hole in the hull. Another charge was set in the aft torpedo compartment.

The *U-111* sank stern first in 266 fathoms.

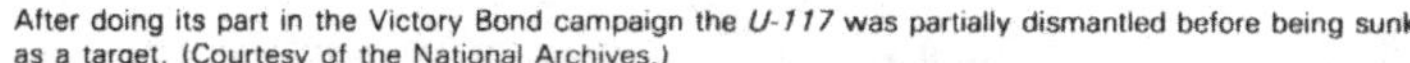

After doing its part in the Victory Bond campaign the *U-117* was partially dismantled before being sunk as a target. (Courtesy of the National Archives.)

Sightseers on the dock await their turn to board the *U-111*. (Courtesy of the Naval Photographic Center.)

U-111's War Activity

As noted in *Shipwrecks of Virginia*, the *U-111* made three war patrols. All three patrols were under the command of Kapitanleutnant Hans Beyersdorff, and took place around the British Isles in 1918.

The first patrol started with a bang and was the most successful, as Beyersdorff sank the 2,346-ton British steamer *Boscastle* with a single torpedo. Though he lingered in the area for nearly a week, he encountered no more targets.

On the second patrol he sank two small targets whose combined tonnage totaled only slightly more than one-quarter the tonnage of the *Boscastle*: the 393-ton Danish motor vessel *Dronning Margrethe*, and the 272-ton Norwegian sailing vessel *Rana*.

The third patrol ended with a whimper. Beyersdorff returned to the *U-111's* home port of Emden without having fired a single shot in anger.

By that time – September 30, 1918 – the war was winding down. Six weeks later, the Kaiser capitulated by signing the Armistice on November 11, a date that is now celebrated as Veterans Day: the end of the greatest war in human history (until World War Two).

PICKLES AND JELLY DIET FOR U.S. CREW FOR THREE DAYS

But Plucky Navy Men on Disabled U Boat Beat Transport to Port

The grit of men of the United States Navy was again revealed today in the story of how four officers and thirty-eight men, on a diet of pockels [sic] and jelly for three days brought the disabled German *U-111* into New York a day ahead of the new steamship with which they had left Brest. The U boat, with which they struggled through a stormy trip to get it here in time for the Victory Loan campaign, is now at the Brooklyn Navy Yard.

Lieut. Commander Garnet Holings, executive officer, told the story of the hardships after Washington had lifted the veil of secrecy that for two days kept reporters from the undersea craft.

The *U-111*, with four officers and thirty-four sailors, left Plymouth April 7, passing Brest two days later, just as the Zeppelin was starting for Hoboken with troops. The Zeppelin, which was built by the North German Lloyd during the war, was turned over by Germany to the allies and allocated to America.

When the Americans, all from American submarines (Lieut. Commander Holings had charge of the American LA-4 [an L-class blimp] fourteen months in the war zone), received the *U-111* at Plymouth they found the starboard main bearings burned out through bad engineering by the Germans rather than to deliberate damaging. Day and night the crew toiled for twelve days, sleeping in shifts of a few hours, to make the engine serviceable.

Throughout the voyage, the men on the *U-111* suffered the hardships involved in travelling on a frail craft in stormy weather and heavy seas. The U boat rolled constantly. At times she made sixteen knots, but usually ten. Always she had to remain on the surface.

DID NOT DARE USE BOTH ENGINES AT SAME TIME

The vessel used each engine alternately only two hours at a time.

"We did not know what would happen if we tried to use them both at the same time," explained Lieut. Commander Holings to-day.

"Three days from New York, off Nantucket Light, the starboard engine went bad. We made the remainder of the trip on one engine. At the same time we ran desperately short of food. In our earnestness in making repairs we had overlooked stocking the boat with sufficient provisions.

"We suddenly discovered that we had only a lot of jelly and pickles and some potatoes that could not be used. We managed to live on that, however. On the last day, as we came near New York, we ran entirely out of water. When we docked we had only enough fuel for five hours' steaming. The men showed the effects of those three days, but were more fatigued from those twelve days' incessant work at Plymouth than by their trials at sea. You see, they were anxious to get the boat there in time for the Victory Loan, and they did.

The day after the *U-111* arrived at the Navy Yard the transport Zeppelin put in at Hoboken.

The *U-111*, which is believed by Navy Yard officials, because of her type and capabilities, to have been one of those that attacked shipping off our coast last year, is one of several German submarines that have been turned over to America by the Allies for exhibition in the Victory Loan campaign in various parts of the country.

WILL TAKE TRIP ALONG NEW ENDLAND [SIC] COAST

The *U-111* will start to-morrow for Portland, Me [Maine], and will be shown at New England ports. The others to be shown are the *U-140*, *UC-97*, *UB-148* [sic] and *UB 88*. These are coming with the tender Bushnell, which carries the records of each boat in the war.

These craft were turned over to the Allies by their German personnel off Harwich in December. Last month they were given to America. Lieut. Commander Freeman A. Daubin was placed in command of the *U-111*. Besides Lieut. Commander Holings the other officers were Ensign M. T. Grubham, engineer officer, and Lieut. W. S. Henry, gunner.

The *U-111* is 240 feet long. She has two deck guns, each 4.1 calibre [sic], stationed fore and aft. There are four bow tubes and two at the stern, with room for twelve torpedoes. She has a maximum speed of nineteen knots on the surface and ten submerged and has a radius of 7,000 miles at ten knots. The engines are Diesel oil burners. On the bow is a steel saw six feet long, for cutting wire netting.

In size, the *U-111* is somewhat like the American S boats. American submarine experts who have examined the German craft admitted today that she contained many improvements over devices in our undersea craft, notably the gyroscopic compass. They pointed out, however, that although Germany's best science had been concentrated in that type of boat, the *U-111* was too complicated in its maze of valves and pipe leads. The arrangement of its devices was described as poor and inferior to the American submersibles. Her periscopes, of which there are three, are higher than those on American vessels. The ventilating system is excellent.

NEWER TYPE OF U BOAT TO ARRIVE HERE SOON

Most of the boats of the type of the *U-111* were based during the war at Kiel and Pota, operating off Ireland, France, Spain and the Mediterranean.

The *U-140* represents the largest type, with displacement of more than 3,000 tons, with a speed of nineteen knots surfaced and nine knots submerged, and a cruising radius of 5,000 miles at six knots.

Officers and crewmembers of the *U-111*. (From the *Evening World*.)

The *UC-97*, due soon, was a mine layer and will be shown at the Great Lakes. She carried eighteen mines, three torpedo tubes, six torpedoes and a three-inch gun.

Though the American officers now in charge of the *U-111* are not acquainted with the war history of that craft, they asserted that when they obtained the submarine they found in it a remarkably accurate chart of English mines.

Also found were letters to and from members of the crew. Some of these contained grammatical English phrases. One scrap of paper had a poem in German, glorying in the exploits off Newport of the *U-53*, which sank three steamships several hours after obtaining provisions and fuel there.

Evening World, April 23, 1919

Non-firing gun practice on the *U-111*.
(Courtesy of the Naval Photographic Center.)

Exuberant crewmembers are happy to be alive after a treacherous crossing of the Atlantic Ocean. (Courtesy of the Naval Photographic Center.)

The Kaiser's U-boats in American Waters

Not only was the *U-111* the first ex-German U-boat to reach the American coast, it beat all the others to the bottom of the ocean, although only temporarily. On June 13, 1921, the minesweeper *Quail* towed the *U-111* out of the Portsmouth Navy Yard. On June 14, the U-boat appeared to be down by the head by about four feet. It remained in that attitude for the rest of the voyage. Upon their arrival at Lynnhaven Roads, on June 16, the *U-111* was secured to a mooring buoy and an inspection was made. A Navy memorandum stated:

"On opening the hatch of the forward torpedo compartment this compartment was found full of water. The wrecking pump of the tug was able to lower the level of this water until it could be seen that a considerable stream was coming from one of the torpedo tubes. The rear door of this tube had been removed at the Navy Yard as had also the hand-wheel for operating the bow door. An inspection of the compartment next astern of the torpedo room showed that there was practically no water in this compartment. No anxiety was felt for the vessel and it was intended to improvise a tube shutter on the morning of 17 June. The *Quail* remained alongside the vessel all night pumping intermittently."

The pump was disconnected in the morning as the *Quail* proceeded to shove off for other duty. The *U-111* began to settle quickly. "An inspection of the compartment next astern showed that some of the wooden plugs in the inner hull of the vessel had come out and that this compartment was also flooding. Two plugs, one of them about six inches in diameter were seen to blow out about this time."

The *Quail* rerigged the towing lines and tried to beach the U-boat. On the way to shore, the *U-111's* bow grounded in five fathoms. Slowly, the stern sank, until the U-boat rested on the bottom with three feet of water over the conning tower.

No salvage equipment was available in the 5th Naval District. It was therefore suggested that the U.S. salvage tug *Falcon* be assigned to raise the U-boat. At that time the *Falcon* was conducting salvage operations on the U.S. submarine *S-5*, off the coast of Delaware, and could not be spared.

The *U-111* was left on the bottom for more than a year. Obviously it missed the gunnery and bombing tests. It also missed the deadline that was prescribed by treaty, but no one complained.

A gas buoy with a red flashing light was placed on the wreck of the *U-111*. Six mooring buoys were set. The *Falcon* arrived over the U-boat on October 1, 1921. Divers went to work in the pitch-black compartments. After a month and a half of hard work, the *Falcon* was called off for other duty. She wintered in New York, where she underwent a refit. It was not until June 1922 that she returned to the site of the *U-111*.

Above: *U-111* in Boston Harbor. (Courtesy of the National Archives.)
Below: *U-111* in a Philadelphia dry-dock. (Courtesy of the National Archives.)

SALVAGING A U-BOAT TO SINK IT

By EDWARD G. MAXWELL

The United States Ship "Falcon," the Navy's Salvage Ship, Which is Equipped with the Most Modern Devices and is Manned by a Crew of Experts, Selected from the Whole Personnel of the Navy

THOUGH equipped with the most modern devices for raising sunken vessels and manned by a crew in which are specialists drafted from the whole navy, the U. S. S. "Falcon," the navy's salvage ship, was two months in floating the ex-German submarine "U-111" which once attempted to cheat the executioner. The teredo, aquatic auger of southern waters, was to blame.

The "U-111" was brought to the United States, following the armistice, with a number of other war vessels which had flown the kaiser's flag until turned over to the allies at Scapa Flow. It was taken to the Norfolk Navy Yard, where the men who design American fighting craft pried around inside it to find out what made the German undersea fleet the terror of the world. In their quest for structural secrets they removed all

Above: Barnacle-Covered Prow of the Ex-German Submarine "U-111," as It Lay in Drydock. Left: The Submarine in Drydock at the Norfolk Navy Yard, Where It was Completely Dismantled to Discover Its Secrets

pipe and with wooden plugs stopped up the holes where the pipe went through

Commander of the United States Ship "Falcon," Standing on the Deck beside the Conning Tower of the Ex-German Submarine "U-111"

the hull. There were 80 outlets, altogether.

Nearly two years ago the "U-111," which was a commerce raider during the war, was towed out from Norfolk in company with the other ex-German vessels, to be sunk in deep water in accordance with the treaty terms. Its companions were destroyed, as scheduled, by bombs dropped from naval airplanes, but the "U-111," a stubborn craft, sank in 40 feet of water while being towed to sea.

The navy knew that the grave into which the submarine had cast itself was not deep enough to satisfy the treaty provisions, but the "Falcon" was busy on other assignments, and it was nearly 18 months before the salvage ship, a converted minesweeper, was ordered to raise the last of the ex-Germans. The sinking of the submarine in shallow water, it was thought, was due to the slipping of one of the wooden plugs, and the "Falcon" was expected to meet no difficulty in again plugging the hole and pumping the craft out so that it would rise. The existence of the teredo was ignored in these calculations.

But during the time the "U-111" had lain on the bottom, the teredo, which is a sort of shellfish with an unappeasable appetite for wood, had cut into sawdust, to the last plug, the 80 stoppers put in while the submarine was in drydock. The "Falcon's" crew, among whom are 18 skilled divers, had to patch up something which was far from being a boat and not so far from being a sieve. When the Navy Department learned the true conditions, all agreed that the "Falcon" had done well in floating the submarine in eight weeks.

On the surface again, the "U-111" enjoyed but a short life. As soon as the patches put in under water by the divers were strengthened to prevent a recurrence of the first accident, the "Falcon" towed it offshore and sank it, with a mine, out beyond the 200-fathom line.

Divers eventually managed to seal the open torpedo tube, and replace the wooden plugs that had popped out of the inner hull. On July 29, the *Falcon* pumped air into the U-boat's compartments, but succeeded in raising only the stern.

On August 4, the *Falcon* towed two pontoons to the wreck site. After much hard work in securing the pontoons to the sunken hull, the *U-111* was finally raised and towed to dry-dock at the Norfolk Navy Yard, on August 14. There the U-boat was repaired well enough so that it could be towed to sea for scuttling.

The *Falcon* departed for the Portsmouth Navy Yard on August 30, with the *U-111* lashed to her starboard side. Aboard the salvage vessel was Mr. H. D. Blaunet, of the Pathe Moving Picture Company. He was assigned the task of recording the sinking on motion picture film.

Once in the open sea, the U-boat was dropped astern of the *Falcon* on a hundred fathoms of wire. The following day, when the *Falcon* reached the prearranged site, a charge was detonated in the forward battery room of the U-boat, blowing a hole in the hull. Another charge was detonated in the aft torpedo compartment.

The *U-111* sank stern first in 266 fathoms, or 1596 feet.

Or did it?

The *U-111* in the Norfolk Navy Yard dry-dock. (Courtesy of the National Archives.)

Before I answer that question, I want to make an insert and include a couple of chapters that will shed some light on the process of shipwreck research: some of which might lead researchers astray, others which make sense only after lengthy thought and discussion. Bear with me.

Shipwreck research requires dedication. A dedicated researcher cannot simply rely on searching the Internet. This is not to say (or write) that primary information cannot be found on the Internet; some can. But a researcher who copies secondhand information is likely to repeat mistakes that the original writer made because his or her research relied on secondary sources.

Some seemingly primary sources may lead a researcher astray. Consider the *Dictionary of American Naval Fighting Ships* (known as DANF). This eight-volume encyclopedia was written by Navy personnel who had access to primary Navy sources in the library of the Naval Historical Center, which is kept at the Washington Navy Yard in Washington, DC. Yet by doing my own primary research from original documents, throughout my career of shipwreck research I have found numerous, even copious mistakes, errors, and misinterpretations.

Consider this entry for the *U-111*:

> **At New York, swarms of tourists, reporters, and photographers roamed throughout the submarine. Navy technicians and civilian shipbuilders also came to try to learn everything they could about German submarine construction in the brief time before *U–111* departed New York for visits to various ports on the Victory bond circuit. For the bond drive, the coasts of the United States and the country's major waterways were divided into five different regions, one for each of the captured U-boats except *U–140*. *U–111* visited ports along the New England coast and received visitors in conjunction with the sales campaign. The submarine completed her assigned itinerary late in the summer of 1919. Following that, she and *UB–148* were subjected to an extensive series of performance tests before being laid up at the Philadelphia Navy Yard. During the summer of 1921, she returned to sea for another series of tests, this time as a target for gunnery and aerial bombardment tests. As a result of those experiments, her battered hulk went to the bottom of the ocean sometime in July 1921.**

Compare the last two sentences with the account that I have given One would hope that, with all the resources available to Navy historians, they would have done a better job of reporting the circumstances of the scuttling. DANF was published by the Naval Historical Center, or as I have sometimes referred to it, the Naval Hysterical Center.

Historycentral.com copied the fate of the *U-111* verbatim, thus perpetuating the Navy account, which is not just inaccurate but totally fictitious. Undoubtedly, others have copied the wrong information from either of these sources. That's why people say, "Don't believe everything you read on the Internet."

But wait! There's more!

DANF online was updated in February 2021: "*U-111* cleared the Norfolk Navy Yard on 30 August 1922, but the following day was opened to the sea, *Falcon* detonating a depth charge next to the boat that then sank in 300 feet of water along the Virginia coast, in proximity to the Winter Quarters [sic, should be singular] Shoal Light Ship."

This is slightly more accurate than the paper DANF entry, at least with respect to dates, but adds confusing and inaccurate information.

Stating that the "*U-111* cleared the Norfolk Navy Yard" implies that it departed under its own power, and not under tow by the *Falcon*.

A depth charge was not detonated "next to the boat." Explosive charges were planted in fore and aft compartments, then detonated.

The boat did not sink in 300 feet of water. It sank in 390 feet of water. But I was the only person who knew the actual depth. So where did the figure 300 originate?

The Winter Quarter Shoal lies fifty miles from the *U-111*. I would hardly call that "in proximity to."

The Winter Quarter Shoal Lightship was discontinued in 1961. It was replaced with a lighted buoy.

By exchanging one inaccuracy for a handful of others, this new entry seems like a case of "one step forward, six steps back."

The gun crew of the *U-111* at practice. (Courtesy of the Naval Photographic Center.)

I did not cover the submarine *R-8* in my Popular Dive Guide Series, nor have I covered it in any of my other shipwreck books. I knew about the wreck, of course, and I had records of her history. But her career and loss were too lackluster to encourage me to waste the time and effort on further research, especially as it was scuttled half a mile deep in the Southern Drill Grounds off the coast of southern Virginia.

According to the *Dictionary of American Naval Fighting Ships*:

R–8

(Submarine No. 85: dp. 569 (surf.), 680 (subm.); l. 186′2″; b. 18′ dr. 14′6″; s. 13.5 k. (surf.), 10.5 k. (subm.); cpl. 34; a. 1 3″, 4 21″ tt.; cl. *R–1*)

R–8 (Submarine No. 85) was laid down 4 March 1918 by the Fore River Shipbuilding Co., Quincy, Mass.; launched 17 April 1919; sponsored by Miss Penelope Potter; and commissioned 21 July 1919, Lt. Comdr. Philip C. Ransom in command.

R–8 fitted out at Boston during the fall of 1919, proceeded to New London 5 December, joined other boats of Submarine Division 9, and continued south for winter exercises in the Gulf of Mexico. She operated out of Pensacola until returning to New England in April. Designated SS–85 in July she departed Newport on 13 September and 2 days later arrived at Norfolk for overhaul prior to transfer to the Pacific Fleet. Sea trials in early April 1921 followed and on the 21st she headed south. Transiting the Panama Canal in May, she arrived at San Pedro, her new homeport, 30 June, and for the next 2 years conducted exercises—individual, divisional and fleet—off the coasts of California and Mexico. On 16 July 1923, she sailed west for Pearl Harbor, her base for almost 8 years, during which she engaged in training and operations with fleet units. In August 1927, she searched for missing Dole Flight Aviators.

Ordered back to the east coast for inactivation in 1930, *R–8* departed Pearl Harbor 12 December, transited the Panama Canal in mid-January 1931, and arrived at Philadelphia 9 February. Decommissioned 2 May, she was berthed at Philadelphia as a unit of the Reserve Fleet until 1936. On 26 February of that year, while still in a state of preservation, she sank. Later raised, she was struck from the Navy list 12 May 1936 and on 19 August she was used as a target vessel for an aerial bombing test. Four near misses with 100 lb. bombs sank her 71 miles off Cape Henry, Va.

DANF neglected to mention that the *R-8* had been involved in two collisions. Neither one resulted in loss of life, but when the submarine overtook and ran down the *Itasca*, the schooner was sunk. Here are the particulars.

The *Itasca* was a 75-ton schooner that was built in 1879 at Cherry Field, Maine. Her home port was Machias, Maine. She measured 72 feet in length, sported a beam of 24 feet, and had a depth of 5 feet.

On August 20, 1920, the *Itasca* was on passage from Newport, Rhode Island to Gloucester, Massachusetts. She was plying the waves off Brenton Reef, Rhode Island, when the three people on board observed the submarine astern and proceeding on a nearly parallel course off the starboard side of the *Itasca*. The submarine was slowly closing the distance as her track also converged with that of the schooner.

When collision became imminent, the *R-8* turned to port "under the schooner's stern and reversed, but a collision occurred."

The *R-8* escaped with minor damage, but the *Itasca's* hull was breached, resulting in her sinking. Although extant records do no state specifically, I presume that the *R-8* rescued the *Itasca's* crew from the water, as *Merchant Vessels of the United States* states that no lives were lost.

There was no doubt about who was at fault for the crash. Yet the Navy stubbornly refused to pay Frank B. Newton, the owner of the *Itasca*, for the loss of his $5,000 vessel. By comparison, today a 72-foot schooner is worth about half a million dollars. Inflation!

According to the Maritime Rules of the Road, an overtaking vessel is responsible for staying out the way of the vessel that she is overtaking. Stated another way, it is not the responsibility of a vessel to get out of the way of an overtaking vessel, but to maintain its course.

Additionally, a sailing vessel *always* has the right of way against a motorized vessel. The reason for this is because a sailing vessel is subject to the vagaries of the wind, whereas a motorized can navigate without regard to the wind. Thus, in order not to contribute to a possible collision, a sailing vessel is *required by law* not to change course in a situation in which collision might be imminent. This is so that the motorized vessel can be assured of the sailing vessel's course while making maneuvers to avoid a collision.

The Rules of the Road are neither arbitrary nor capricious. They are based on pure logic and reason. Thus, the Navy did not have a chance of winning a case like this in court. Yet the Navy forced Newton to file a suit in order to obtain reimbursement for his loss: money that was rightfully his.

The Navy managed to drag out the case for *six years*. At last, on April 3, 1926, the final opinion of the court was rendered.

Judge Brewster's summation made it sound as if he was furious that the Navy had not paid Newton immediately, instead of allowing such an open and shut case – a "no brainer" in modern lingo – to continue for half a decade: "I find that the submarine was at fault and that she negligently and recklessly ran into the schooner and failed, being the overtaking vessel, to keep out of her way, and that said carelessness and negligence were the causes of the collision."

Oops!The crushed conning tower of the *R-8*. (Courtesy of the Naval Photographic Center.)

The *R-8* was certainly reckless, but the situation was undoubtedly not wreckless!

Meanwhile, on October 5, 1925, the *R-8* was involved in another collision. This time there was no lawsuit because the collision occurred between two Navy vessels.

"The U.S. submarine *R-8,* while running submerged at a depth of 26 feet, rammed the U. S. S. *Widgeon* off Pearl Harbor. The *R-8* was making an unseen attack on the *Widgeon* which was running an unknown zigzag course and at an unknown speed. The commanding officer of the submarine attempted to avoid the collision by diving under

Another view of the crushed conning tower of the *R-8*. (Courtesy of the Naval Photographic Center.)

The *Widgeon* at the Sun Shipbuilding Company, Chester, Pennsylvania, on July 26, 1918, the day before she was commissioned. (Courtesy of the Naval Photographic Center.)

the *Widgeon* but failed to reach the required depth on account of the proximity of the vessels. The entire bridge structure and both periscopes of the *R-8* were carried away or damaged beyond repair, but control was not lost and the submarine came to the surface about 1 minute after the collision. (No lives lost.)"

I hope that the Navy has learned by now that diving under a vessel as a way to avoid collision was not recommended.

The *Widgeon* was built in 1918 by the Sun Shipbuilding and Dry Dock Company, which was located along the Delaware River in Chester, Pennsylvania. The minesweeper measured 187 feet in length, boasted a beam of 37 feet, and had a draft of 13 feet. Her displacement tonnage was calculated as 1,400 tons.

After the war, she was converted to a salvage vessel, and was operating in that capacity at the time the *R-8* rammed into her. In 1936, she was reclassified at a submarine rescue vessel. She was sold for scrap in 1948.

Under the entry for *Widgeon*, DANF conveniently neglected to mention her collision with the *R-8*. In case you haven't noticed, DANF has a habit of extolling the virtues of U.S. Navy vessels while ignoring their flaws and faults.

By 1936, the R-class design had long since been superseded, first by the S-class – whose design was based on features of the six German U-boats of the Ex-German Submarine Expeditionary Force, which Navy engineers examined in detail – then by a series of designs of submarines that were larger, faster, and more efficient than the previous classes. After a lackluster career, the *R-8* was scuttled by means of aerial bombardment. Even as a wreck, the *R-8* was insignificant because the submarine had no historical value.

Yet, after the *R-8* was (supposedly) side-scanned and a press release was issued – on or about December 10, 2020 – newspapers outdid themselves in employing unwarranted yellow journalism to describe the magnitude of the event. Here are a few examples:

"The discovery of *R-8* would be historically significant."

"WW1-era U.S submarine found frozen in time on ocean floor."

"If the discovery is verified, it would be one of the few missing American submarines left in East Coast waters."

"Captain Eric Takakjian and D/V *Tenacious* Captain Joe Mazraani have been working on the *R-8* Project for many years."

"Divers haven't been able to reach the submarine yet, but Atlantic Wreck Salvage is confident based on sonar and location data as well as historical records the wreck they found is indeed *R-8*, according to the company."

"The sonar data leaves little doubt that the *R-8* has been located. The submarine in the [side-scan] image is the correct length, width and height. One set of prominent features of the R-class subs visible in the scan image is the spray rail configuration on the conning tower."

"Salvage co. believes it's found submarine wreckage off Ocean City."

"The World War 1 vintage submarine is reported to be intact and sitting upright on the ocean floor making it one of the few American submarines resting in diveable East Coast waters that had yet to be located.

"According to available information, the found submarine, which dates back to World War 1, is virtually intact and sits flush on its keel."

"Captain Ted Green assisted the research team by providing information about potential targets he had gathered throughout his years captaining the dive boat *OC Diver*."

"Discovering a submarine is so rare it is particularly exciting." (I know this for a fact because I have discovered five submarines: *Tarpon*, *U-140*, *UB-148*, *U-117*, and *U-2513*.)

"The discovery of any new vessel is exciting."

Note the conning tower low in the water in the horizontal center of the photograph. (Courtesy of the Naval Photographic Center.)

With this final quote I whole-heartedly agree. I have found that discovering even a lowly barge or fishing vessel is exciting, the reason being that no one has ever seen it or explored it before. Perhaps only a dedicated wreck-diver can understand such a sentiment, but there it is.

Despite the hype and hoopla, there is also a kernel of doubt about identifying a shipwreck without seeing it or recovering an item that has the vessel's name on it. Perhaps there is even a whole cob. To be fair, this seldom happens. I have often said and written that in many cases a shipwreck is identified not by finding an artifact with a name on it, but by a preponderance of evidence. To obtain this evidence and to authenticate a wreck's identity usually requires repeated visits to the site.

As one newspaper noted, "The *Tenacious* team isn't revealing the sub's exact location until they get a chance, during the June-July weather window, to dive and see her with their own eyes."

And there's the rub. To my knowledge, the "*Tenacious* team" (alias Atlantic Wreck Salvage, alias Joe Mazraani) has never revealed the location of any shipwreck that it has claimed to have discovered. This makes it difficult or nearly impossible to obtain independent confirmation, which is the foundation of scientific discovery. Furthermore, as of this writing, to my knowledge the "*Tenacious* team" has yet to "dive and see her with their own eyes." Nor has the *Tenacious* team returned for any other reason.

Despite these caveats, I naively believe in giving people the benefit of the doubt. I accepted the identity on a provisional basis, and conducted immediate research with that in mind.

The historical position of the *R-8's* scuttling site places the wreck in water that is half a mile deep. That depth is beyond the crush limit of all but a few side-scan sonar units or remotely operated vehicles; that is, those that cost less than hundreds of thousands or millions of dollars to manufacture. And this is to say nothing of the length and weight of the connecting cable that is necessary to reach that depth. But . . .

. . . if the wreck were found about eight miles westward of its reported position, the depth of water would be only 500 feet. This is within the bounds of possibility. Let me explain.

In today's world, when people think of accuracy in location, they think in terms of the Global Positioning System (GPS), which can pinpoint drivers and hikers to within a hundred feet. But in 1936, when the *R-8* was scuttled, the only method of establishing a position at sea was with a sextant, a chronometer, and a book of mathematical tables. Sun sightings were taken at sunrise, noon, or sunset. Any position between those sightings was obtained by "dead reckoning." A dead reckoning position was obtained by estimating the combination of speed, drift, and wind. Speed was approximated by engine revolutions or a taffrail log. Drift was a correction based on the perceived speed and direction of current and tide, as was wind. If a sighting was obscured by an overcast sky – for hours or days on end – the inaccuracy of dead reckoning grew larger and larger.

Good accuracy was considered to be one to three miles. Acceptable accuracy could be three to five miles. Eight miles was a stretch but not without precedent.

Consider the historical inaccuracy concerning the *Octavian*. The Allied Assessors placed the wreck off the coast of Nova Scotia because they believed that it had been torpedoed by the *U-203*. In my research files I found a mention that the *Octavian* may have been torpedoed by the *U-123*, which was known to have been operating in the area where divers found the putative *Octavian*. I happened to have an English translation of the deck log of the *U-123*. There I found an entry that it had torpedoed an unidentified vessel on the night of January 17, 1942: a position that lay less than half a mile from the wreck site. This site was 600 miles from the site that was given by the Allied Assessors.

I used to blame the Allied Assessors for the number of mistake they made. Then I learned that they did not have access to Ultra. Ultra was a top secret decryption team who intercepted Nazi radio transmissions which were then decoded so that U-boats could be tracked and their positions pinpointed on a plotting board that occupied an entire wall that stood twenty feet high in the Secret Room adjacent to the Submarine Tracking Room.

At the conclusion of hostilities with Nazi Germany, British intelligence units microfilmed all the U-boat deck logs and made copies for the United States. These copies are now accessible from the National Archives in College Park, Maryland.

Then the Allies created the Assessment Committee whose monumental task was to determine which U-boat sank which Allied vessel, and which Allied warship sank which U-boat.

But, the Assessment Committee was not given access to Ultra decrypts. Furthermore, the Assessment Committee was not told of the *existence* of Ultra decrypts. This is equivalent to taking a math quiz in which a student is tasked with finding the correct answer to a problem in which some of the numbers were withheld.

Granted that this was an exceptional case under different circumstances, but it goes to show that historical records are not always accurate. I have a number of historical positions for the *Olinda*. They form a triangle whose legs range as much as sixty miles in length. I will return to this subject later in this chronology.

Aside from historical inaccuracies, errors in dead reckoning can easily be introduced by miscalculations of the speed, drift, or wind, or all of the above. I am aware of a large number of shipwrecks whose actual locations are miles, or tens of miles, from their historical location.

According to one newspaper account about the *R-8's* discovery, the *Tenacious* team spent three days towing a side-scan sonar unit in a failed search for the American submarine. "Then, on the first day of a second trip, came the moment when they saw something big on the monitors." After enhancing and reviewing the "something big," the team claimed that the object was the *R-8*.

Ted Green was credited as one of the research team, although in what capacity was not mentioned. He operated the dive boat *O.C. Diver* out of Ocean City, Maryland. He and I were good friends. I have done a great deal of diving with Ted over the years: some on the *Andrea Doria* as my dive buddy, but most off his own boat. He had a host of numbers that he wanted to explore. Once I went with him on a weeklong trip off

Virginia to search for and dive on unexplored sites. As I later learned but then only suspected, he had furnished the GPS numbers for the wreck that the *Tenacious* team visited on the first day of the second trip, and which they called the *R-8*.

This begs the question: why was the *Tenacious* team dragging a side-scan sonar unit for three days if they already had the numbers?

What also bothered me about this discovery was the discrepancy between the historical location of the *R-8* (71 miles off Cape Henry, Virginia, which was south of the approaches to the Chesapeake Bay) and press release headlines or textual statements claiming that the *R-8* wreck site lay off Ocean City, Maryland. This discrepancy made me wonder why the *Tenacious* team started its search for the *R-8* in an area that lay so far away from its historical location: a distance of some seventy miles!

Not only that, but if the boat was docked in Ocean City, as the newspapers claimed, the distance to the historical location was a *hundred* miles from the dock. It would have made more sense to move the boat to Virginia Beach, Virginia instead of Ocean City, Maryland.

Nonetheless, I still adhered to my stance that the *Tenacious* crew had side-scanned the *R-8*, no matter where it lay, not only because they said they had done so, but because they claimed that the dimensions of the side-scanned hull matched the actual dimensions of R-class submarines. Circumstantial evidence for sure, but shipwreck identification is often circumstantial. Plus, there aren't many sunken submarines compared with the total number of shipwrecks.

Dare I suggest or imply that reporters might misstate or misrepresent or scramble facts, or sometimes even ignore them altogether? Not I.

There was another curiosity that I could not get out of my mind: For comparison purposes, some newspapers presented side-scan sonar images that the *Tenacious* team provided, along with historic photographs of an unnamed (or unnumbered) submarine sporting "conning tower spray rails," with arrows indicating both the conning tower on the wreck and the conning tower on the historic photograph. These images were supposed to show conformity between the wreck and the *R-8*. Yet the unnamed (or unnumbered) submarine had a conning tower that had the appearance of an upright funnel with five protruding ridges stacked one atop the other. Although some R-class submarines possessed such contrivances, the *R-8* did not . . . and neither does the submarine in the side-scan sonar image. They are totally unalike.

When the *Tenacious* team provided a close-up photograph of a conning tower of an R-class submarine, for some reason they provided one of the *R-17* instead of the *R-8*. Now there were three conning tower images: one of the wreck, one of the *R-17*, and one of the unnamed (or unnumbered) submarine. All three looked different from each other.

Yet none of the newspaper writers mentioned these facts. Perhaps they didn't notice. Or perhaps I was seeing things that were not there.

These two photos of R-class conning towers were used by AWS to compare with the side-scan sonar images of the wreck site. I cannot display the side-scan images because they are copyrighted. The topside images that I snipped off the Internet are out of copyright, and are now in the public domain.

Note that the conning tower structures differ greatly. The photograph above was used to demonstrate the teardrop shape. The photograph at left was used to demonstrate the spray rails. The spray rails are not recognizable on the published side-scan image, which was printed at the size of a postage stamp.

Twenty-seven R-class submarines were constructed. As far as I can determine, only six or seven of them (documentation differs) were either fitted or retrofitted with spray rails. *R-8* was not one of them.

For real-life comparisons, look at the two lower photographs on the facing page. The bottom one shows a close-up of the conning tower of the *R-8* and several of her sister subs in May 1920. The photograph above it was taken during the aerial bombardment, when the *R-8* was scuttled. I enlarged the image and flipped it horizontally so it could be compared with the bottom image.

The image above is a screen shot taken from the video footage that Ross Baxter took on June 22, 2022, when he guided his ROV across the deck of the *Olinda* wreck. Note that the conning tower is far smaller than the conning tower that is shown in the various *R-8* images. Neither does its configuration match any of the *R-8* conning tower configurations. This is compelling evidence that the *Olinda* wreck was not the wreck of the *R-8* (nor of the *Olinda*).

I had several edges over the Tenacious team: I had been doing nearly fulltime shipwreck research since 1980. Because of this, I already knew where the *R-8* was supposed to have been scuttled. And for forty years I had known that the scuttling location of the *U-111* lay some three and a half miles from the *Olinda* wreck. All that I required was to assemble the pieces of this underwater puzzle.

Over the next few weeks and into January 2021, I pondered over the *R-8* issue with increasing skepticism. Rusty Cassway tried to convince me that the *Tenacious* team had not side-scanned the submarine off Cape Henry, Virginia, but off Ocean City, Maryland. He had heard by word of mouth that Ocean City was where the *Tenacious* had docked when it was not at sea and supposedly searching for the *R-8.* So perhaps the reporters were not fabricating evidence after all.

Yet the distance between Ocean City and the historical site of the *R-8* was a hundred miles: a long way to travel on a daily basis. Not that the *Tenacious* did not possess the range to travel that far and back, but because it would have made more sense to move the boat to a port that was located closer to the side-scan sonar site, such as Virginia Beach, Virginia, in order to save fuel costs and running time.

On a later phone call, Cassway told me that he had now heard by word of mouth that the location where the *Tenacious* team had side-scanned the submarine was known by local commercial anglers as the *Olinda* wreck. My memory suddenly clicked. This was the same site as the one for which Ted Green had given the coordinates to me two years earlier.

Zimbra **ggentile@ptd.net**

Olinda numbers

From : Ted green <tedgreen22@yahoo.com> Wed, Apr 11, 2018 01:21 PM
Subject : Olinda numbers
To : gary@ggentile.com

Olinda 37 **47 .268** **74 11 .873**

Ted Green

Out of curiosity, I pulled Ted Green's email from my *Olinda* folder, – the email with the *Olinda* wreck numbers – laid the appropriate offshore chart on the floor, and went directly to the spot where I had already marked the *Olinda* wreck. I noted the same interesting fact that I had noted before but had since forgotten – a fact that was now more meaningful: that the *Olinda* wreck site lay only three and a half miles from where I had marked the *U-111's* position some forty years earlier, when Ken Clayton and I had begun to research and dive on the Billy Mitchell Wrecks.

The prior time I did this I was intrigued. This time I was startled!

That was the moment at which I identified the wreck site of the putative *R-8* as the *U-111*. As the saying goes, "The rest is history."

Or it should be history. In case there are any doubts, I will present the succeeding facts and proofs in detail.

When I compared the *Tenacious* team's actual side-scan sonar image from a press release, with a photograph of the *R-8*'s conning tower from a historical photograph, and examined them closely, I could clearly see that the conning tower of one did not match the conning tower of the other. Before I got too excited, I reminded myself that structural alterations often occurred throughout a vessel's career. I did not know the exact configuration of the *R-8's* conning tower at the time of her scuttling because sea spray and partial submersion caused by the aerial bombardment disguised some of the structure in the photograph that was taken at the time of a bomb strike. Plus, the side-scan sonar image that was reproduced with the article was not particularly clear.

Then I went to a different filing cabinet to pull out my *U-111* folder.

It wasn't there!

Frantically, I searched through the entire drawer, figuring that I must have misfiled it. No matter how hard I searched – not only in that drawer but in several adjacent drawers and filing cabinets whose contents were similar – I still couldn't find it.

At first I was distraught. As I slowly regained my calm, I remembered that I had published the photographs in *Shipwrecks of Virginia.* I opened the book to page 190. Instantly I saw that the sloped conning tower of the *U-111* matched perfectly the sloped conning tower of the *Tenacious* team's side-scan sonar images.

The revelation was clear in my mind. The putative *R-8* was in reality the *U-111*, displaced in both position and depth.

The loss of my *U-111* folder was not a complete disaster. I replaced my photographs faster and easier than it had taken me to obtain them the first time, when I had to physically visit the National Archives and the Naval Photographic Center in Washington, DC. Now I just visited the DANF website and not only recovered my lost photographs but found others that had been accessioned since I had last researched the *U-111*. The loss of the *Falcon's* deck log was not really a loss because the only useful information it contained were the depth and location, both of which I had published in the book and pinpointed on my chart.

The only information that I was missing were the documents that had supported the text in the *U-111* chapter. Had I been a grad student who needed to show sources in order to pass a course or obtain a higher degree, I would have been crushed. But as I was a freelance author and had already used that documentation to write the chapter, I no longer needed the source materials. They had served their purpose.

I called Cassway and gave him the news somewhat like this: "If you go to the *Olinda* wreck, don't be surprised if you find a U-boat instead of a freighter." Even though I was absolutely certain that my identification was correct, I did not want to give him unequivocal assurance. After I explained the reasoning behind my pronouncement, he did not appear to be overwhelmed by my identification. Not that he disagreed with me; he just didn't seem to be as exuberant as I expected.

I looked at the *U-111* as the last undiscovered World War One U-boat on the American eastern seaboard. He seemed to have accepted it as a good theory, but not much more than that.

A postcard picture view of several R-class submarines. Note the conning tower size and configuration.

I thought there would be a mad rush to visit the wreck, despite the depth of 390 feet, if only to confirm its identity. Yet I could understand Cassway's apathy: the wreck was too deep for him to dive. But he did share my *U-111* "theory" with Ben Roberts. He was an expert side-scan sonar operator who owned his own boat and side-scan sonar unit (which he built himself).

Roberts was a different kind of shipwreck explorer. Whereas most wreck-divers want to see and touch a shipwreck firsthand, Roberts' primary focus was in obtaining detailed side-scan sonar images of them. He had already side-scanned some five hundred shipwrecks off the East Coast, from Massachusetts to Virginia. His plan for the summer of 2021 centered on side-scanning the Billy Mitchell Wrecks, among many others, as 2021 was the centennial of their sinking.

This is not to say that he wasn't a shipwreck diver also. He certainly was. He dived on many of the wrecks that he side-scanned. He was also an experienced mixed-gas diver, and had been down to wrecks as deep as 280 feet. At this phase of his shipwreck career, he found it more satisfying to side-scan them, and to share his images with the wreck-diving community through his website, which went by the name Eastern Search & Survey. Google it.

Roberts was curious about my "theory" of the identity of the *U-111* but was not convinced that it was true. At this point I must yield the floor to Ben Roberts as we follow his chronology of events, not only because he compiled the chronology, but also because I was not part of some of the events that followed. Although I am still conducting shipwreck research, and I am still writing shipwreck books, I have quit diving. Thus, my involvement with in-water wreck exploration is largely vicarious.

According to Ben Roberts, "The *U-111* was excluded [from my 2021 side-scan sonar survey] because the consensus at the time was that it rested in waters too deep (˜1,600') for my equipment – and I was not yet convinced by Gentile's theory that the *Olinda* wreck nearby (thought to be the *R-8* but was actually *U-111*) had been misidentified."

Fair enough.

Roberts side-scanned all eight Billy Mitchell Wrecks in a single day!

I wish Clayton and I could have done that in 1990. It would have saved us a great deal of search time. But we had to find the wrecks one at a time because we didn't know their locations until after we discovered them all.

Roberts also side-scanned a slew of other sites, ending the year with a total of 191 sites. This huge project occupied most of his ocean time throughout the summer. He was mostly checking hang numbers, especially those that appeared as clusters where more than one fishing vessel "hung" on something. As he was traveling from one cluster to another in sequence with regard to proximity, he drove over the wreck of one cluster that was so large, and stood so high above the seabed, that he almost struck it with the towfish. Only quick maneuvering enabled him to avoid a collision that could have resulted in a damaged or lost towfish: an expensive piece of equipment and not easily replaceable.

He circled back to side-scan the object that turned out to be a shipwreck. Later, at home, after he downloaded his data, he realized that he had side-scanned the *Olinda*.

The true *Olinda*.

Or had he?

The *R-8* spent five years at the Philadelphia Navy Yard, from 1931 until 1936, "in a state of preservation." She sank at her mooring on February 26, 1936. This is how she appeared after she was raised and towed into drydock. She was struck from the Navy list on May 12, 1936, then scuttled on August 20, 1936 by means of aerial bombardment. It took only four misses with 100-pound bombs to sink her. You will notice that the hull and conning tower are not in their original pristine condition. (Courtesy of the National Archives.)

R-8 underway (Courtesy of the National Archives)

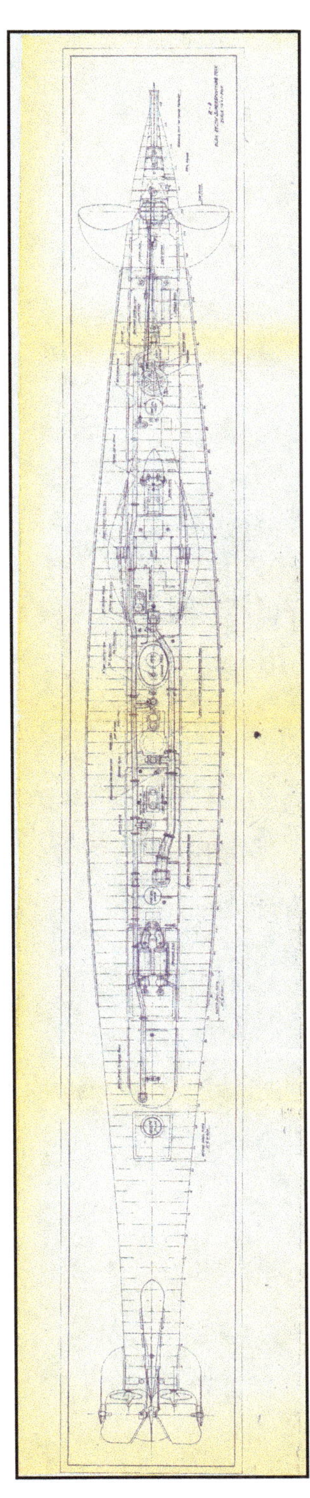

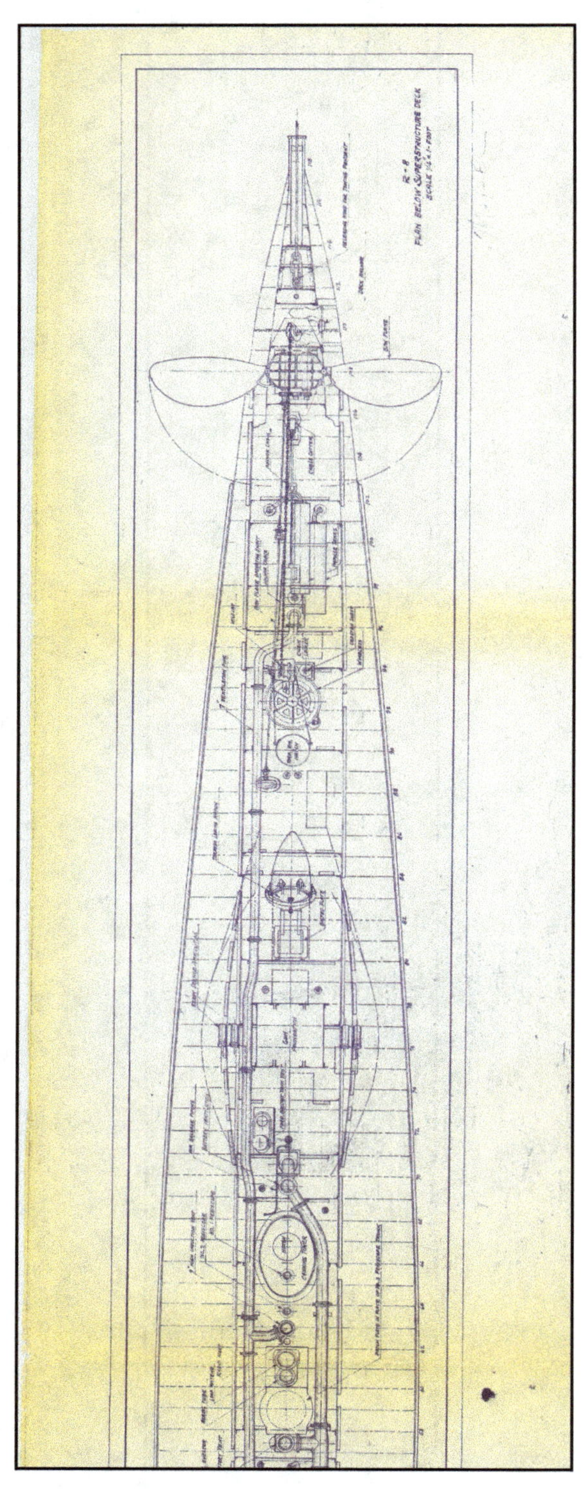

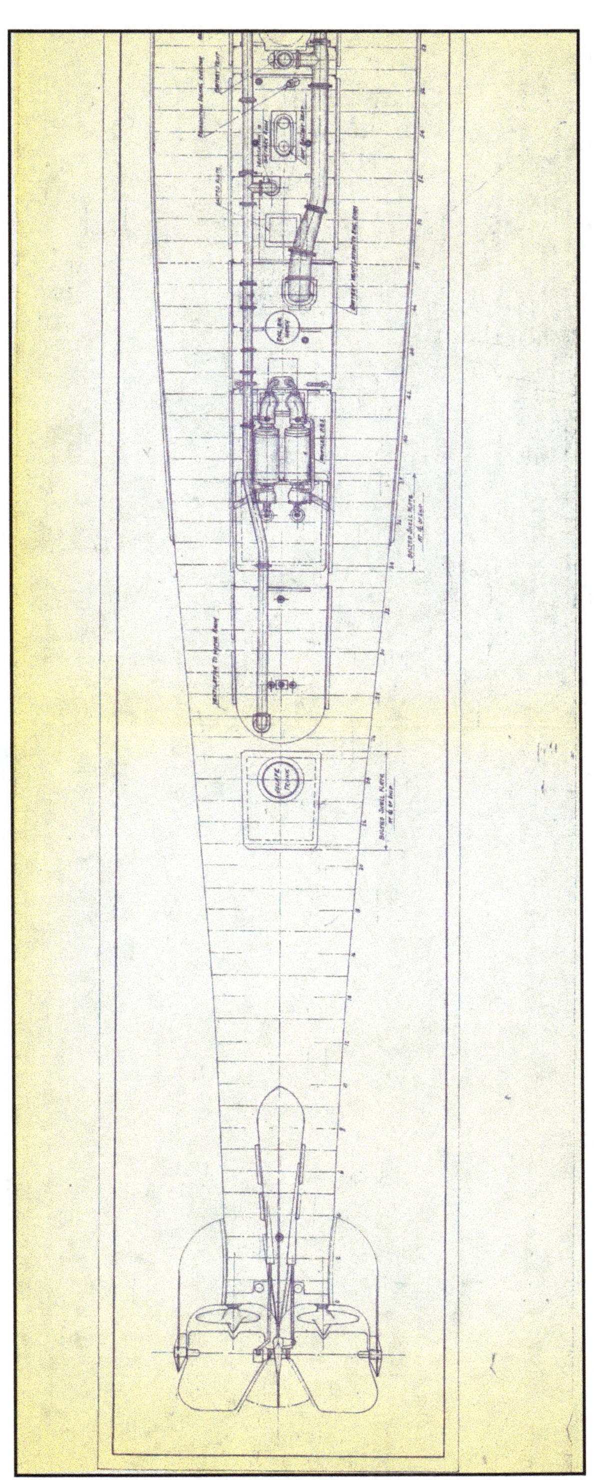

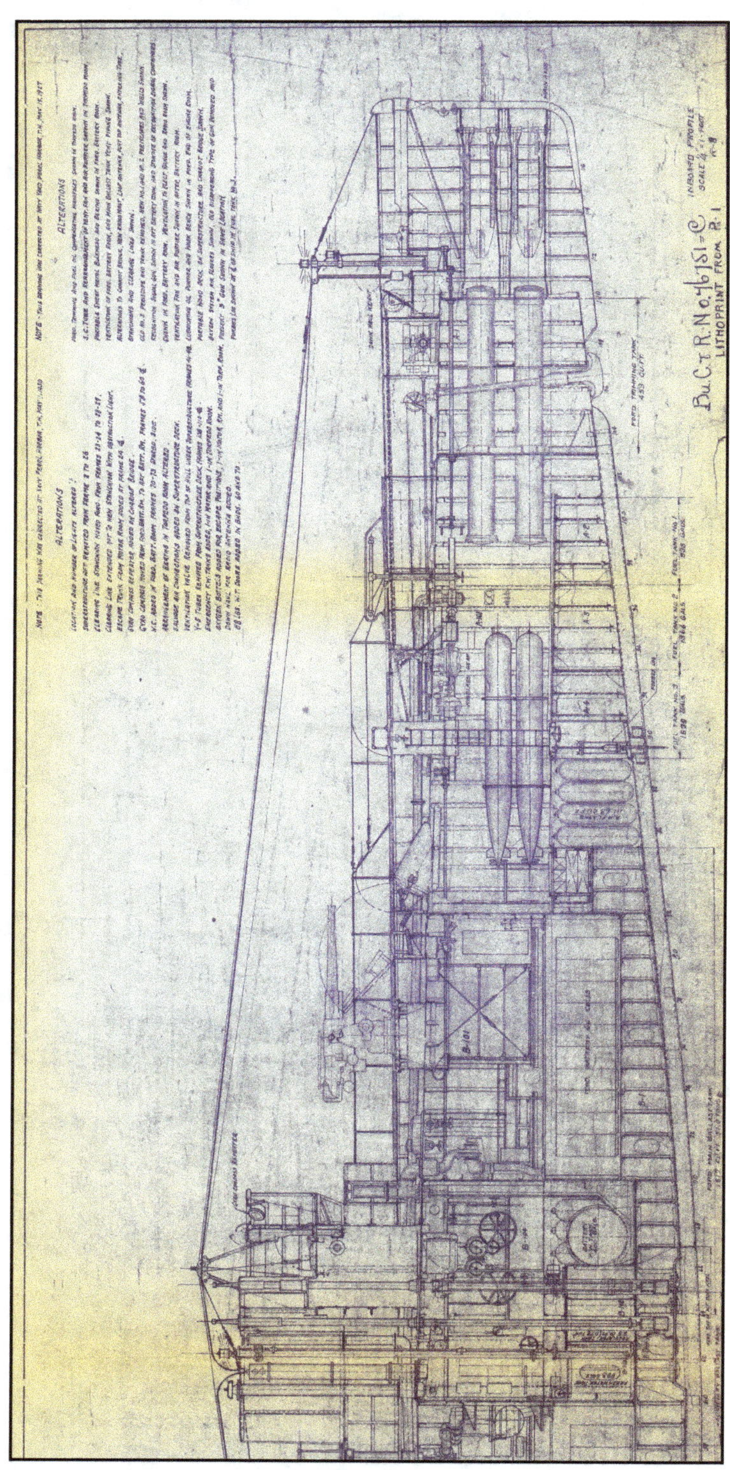

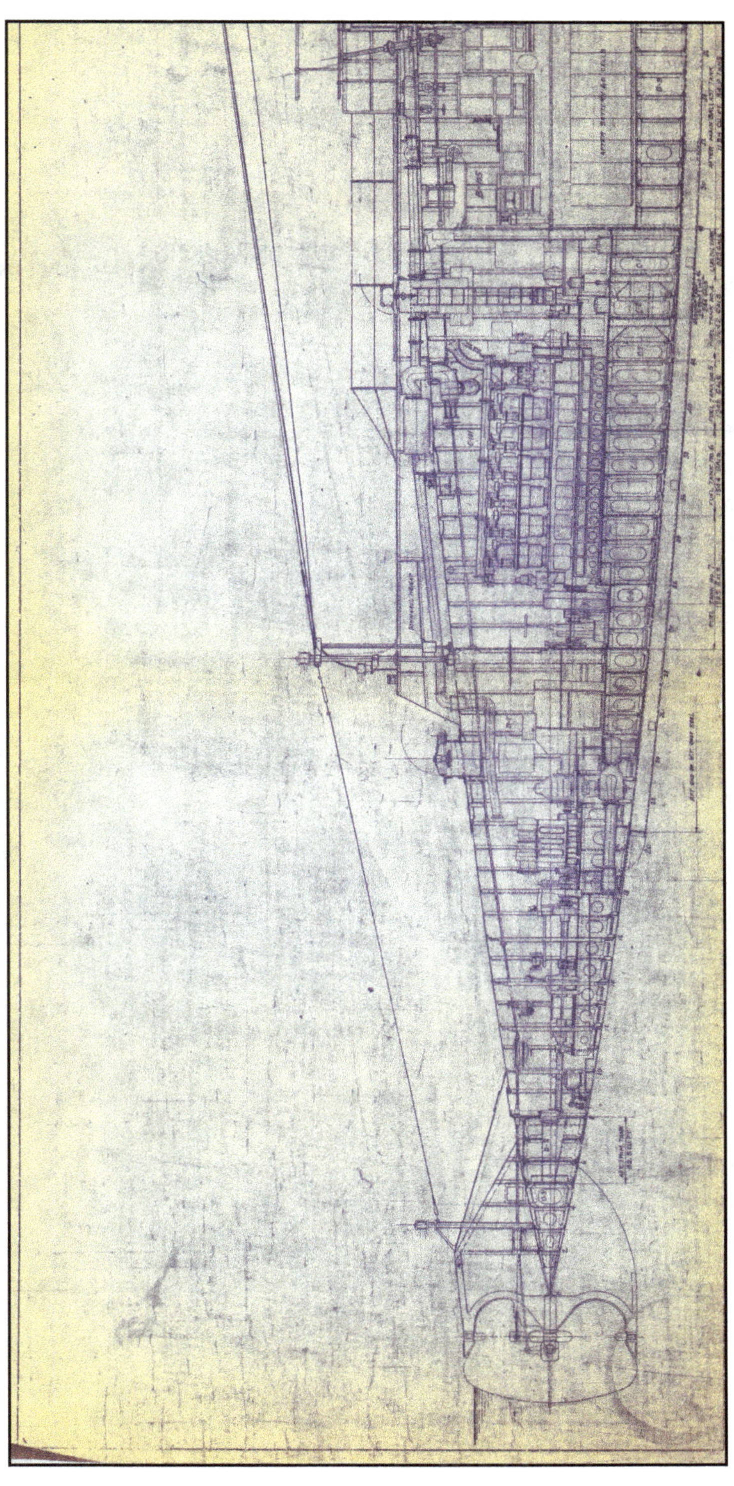

R-8 In Dry-dock (Courtesy of the National Archives)

2732 - U.S. NAVY YARD, NORFOLK, VA. OCT, 6-1920.
DRYDOCK NO.4 - SUBMARINES R.1. TO R.10. INC.
TARGETS 43, 45, 53 & 60.

R-8 Moored (Courtesy of the Naval Photographic Center)

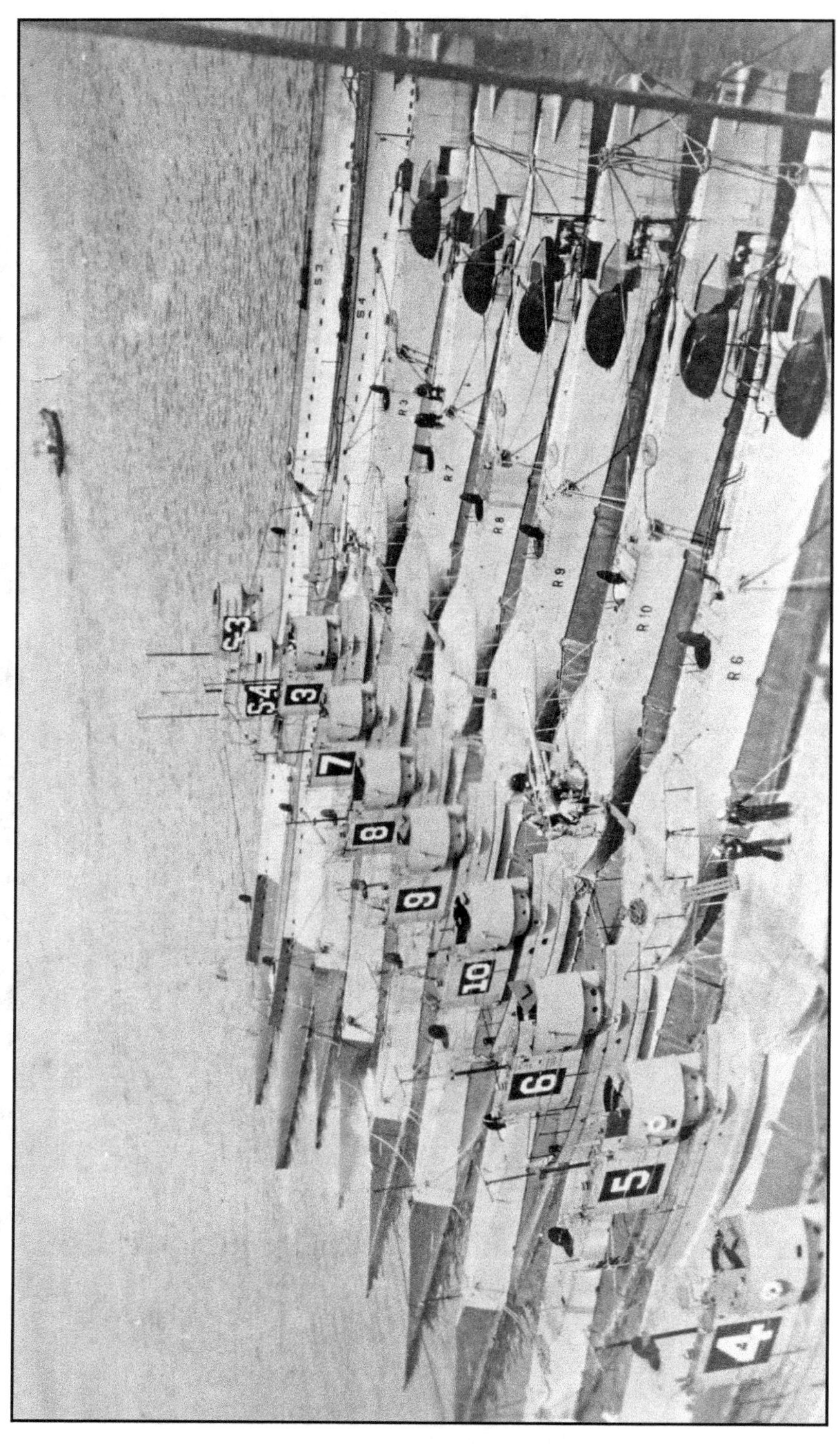

R-8 Alongside USS Camden (Courtesy of the Naval Photographic Center)

The *Olinda* as the *Cara*. Note the vertical wooden stakes that prevent the deck cargo of lumber from falling overboard. (From the author's collection.)

OLINDA

Built: 1905 Sunk: February 18, 1942
Previous names: *Kennemerland*, *Cara* Depth: Unknown
Gross tonnage: 4,053 Dimensions: 359′ × 50′ × 17′
Type of vessel: Freighter Power: Coal-fired steam
Builder: W. Hamilton & Co., Ltd., Port Glasgow, Scotland
Owner: Compania Carbonifera Rio Grandense
Port of registry: Rio de Janeiro, Brazil
Cause of sinking: Torpedoed by *U-432* (Kapitanleutnant Schultze)
Location: 37-30 North 75-00 West

By February 1942 the U-boat campaign off the U.S. east coast was well underway. Swept up in the hostilities were ships of neutral nations. Brazil was trying hard to stay out of the war but wanted to continue commerce with the United States. Brazil's strained diplomatic relations with Germany were not mitigated by a U-boat offensive that failed to recognize neutrality flags.

February 15 found the Brazilian freighter *Buarque* off North Carolina, on a voyage from Rio de Janeiro to New York. The ship was unarmed, fully lighted, and flying the national ensign under the beam of a searchlight. Nevertheless, she was torpedoed and sunk by the *U-432*. Brazil was thrown into an uproar that had not even come close to dying down when Schultze found the *Olinda* plying the same route three days later.

Large Brazilian flags painted on the *Olinda's* steel hull reflected the noonday sun. Her holds were filled with cocoa beans, coffee, and vegetable oil. Due to radio silence her crew was unaware that Germany was not respecting the laws of neutrality. As the freighter lumbered northward some thirty miles off Parramore Island, the bridge watch suddenly noticed a

The *Olinda* as the *Kennemerland*, at Montevideo, Uruguay on May 2, 1931. (Photo by Raul Maya, courtesy of William Schell.)

surfaced submarine some two miles to port. To their horror, they saw that the sub's forward deck gun was manned.

A moment later a gun shell screamed toward the *Olinda*, fell short, and exploded with a splash. Two more followed and also fell short. Since the freighter moved at a speed of only eight knots, the U-boat quickly overtook her; the next three shots were more accurate, tearing away the radio antenna and pummeling the superstructure.

Captain Jacob Benemond ordered abandon ship. With her engines stopped the *Olinda* soon lost way, and the crew hustled to evacuate the sitting target. The port lifeboat got away first. The U-boat then approached it and took off radio operator Francisco Nogueira, who was taken below, photographed, and questioned. He was returned to his lifeboat. The *U-432* turned its attention to the *Olinda's* starboard lifeboat, by this time standing clear of the damaged freighter.

Captain Benemond was taken aboard the U-boat; he was interrogated thoroughly about the *Olinda's* cargo, port of departure, and destination. Unlike the *Buarque*—which had been torpedoed at night without warning, and which sank without communication between her crew and the U-boat—there could be no doubt that the *Olinda* was a neutral vessel. The ship's papers remained on the bridge and could have been secured if Schultze did not believe Captain Benemond's story.

Nevertheless, after Captain Benemond was released the U-boat backed three hundred off the *Olinda's* starboard beam, trained the deck gun, and blasted the hull at the water line. When an additional twenty shots failed to sink the vessel, Schultze fired a torpedo into the motionless freighter at point blank range.

Then came the drone of a patrol plane, attracted to the scene by flames licking off the *Olinda's* superstructure. The U-boat dived. The pilot of the plane spotted the lifeboats floating in the debris field, and dropped a life belt inscribed, "HELP COMING." Help, however, was a long time getting there.

The plane tried to alert a nearby ship of the plight of the *Olinda's* crew, but without success. A second plane sent to help did no better. Darkness settled over the smooth sea. During the night the lifeboats drifted apart due to wind and current. Twenty-three men were crammed into each boat; the cold was insufferable.

Dawn of a new day brought rescue vessels on the prowl. At 0730 the U.S. destroyer *Dallas* (DD-199) hove into view of the first lifeboat, and rescued all personnel. An hour later the *Dallas* spotted the other lifeboat. All forty-six men were saved; only a few suffered superficial injuries.

The wreck of the *Olinda* has not been located. At first hand it would seem to lie in about one hundred feet of water some thirty miles east of Parramore Island. However, a 1944 wreck survey conducted by the U.S. Coast Guard cutter *Gentian* failed to find any trace of the sunken freighter in the listed position.

A thorough examination of archival documents indicate general disagreement of where she actually went down. The *Olinda's* chief officer and second mate placed the sinking at 37-30N/74-10W; both were on watch during the initial attack. The army plane that spotted the flaming vessel reported her position as 37-55N/74-00W; it was flying a dead reckoning course out of Mitchell Field. The plane from Langley Field gave the burning ship's position as 37-38N/74-00W; he also reported seeing three lifeboats with approximately ten men in each. The *Dallas* picked up one lifeboat at 37-40N/74-13W, the second at 37-40N/74-23W, and in her combat report backtracked their drift to a probable sinking location of 37-30N/75-00W. (This position is also verified by German records.) The final ONI (Office of Naval Intelligence) report summarized the attack position as 37-30N/74-00W, with the caveat, "Last sighted afire on 100-fathom. Presumed to have drifted to sea before sinking."

The distance between the inshore position and the offshore position is about sixty miles, the difference north to south some thirty miles, the difference in depth about 5,000 feet. That is a pretty big triangle for a search grid.

Loss Committee Bulletin No.562 of the American Cargo War Risk Reinsurance Exchange cared nothing about the *Olinda's* actual location. In the conduct of business, "The Committee has confirmed that claims per this vessel can be considered as resulting from war perils," and authorized the payment for cargo insured against war risk in the amount of $914,858.

Kapitanleutnant Heinz-Otto Schultze went on the sink the *Azalea City*, *Norlavore*, and *Marore*, all within the confines of the Eastern Sea Frontier, before returning home triumphant. His next war cruise took him to the coast of New England where he sank only two small fishing boats—the *Ben and Josephine* (102 tons) and the *Aeolus* (41 tons). On March 11, 1943, after torpedoing the British destroyer HMS *Harvester* in the North Atlantic, the *U-432* was sunk by the RF *Aconit*. Twenty-six crewmen were killed, twenty were captured.

Olinda (From the author's collection)

(Courtesy of the Naval Photographic Center.)

(Courtesy of the Naval Photographic Center.)

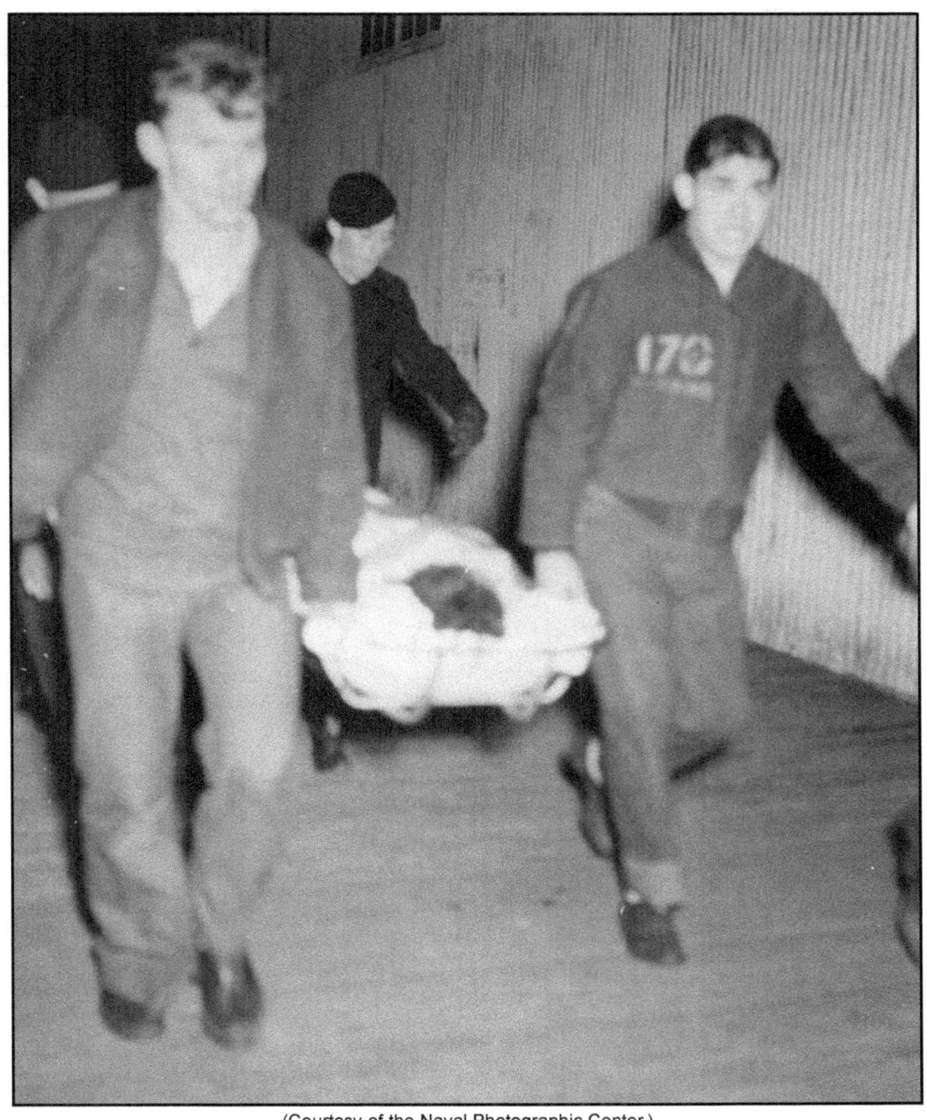

(Courtesy of the Naval Photographic Center.)

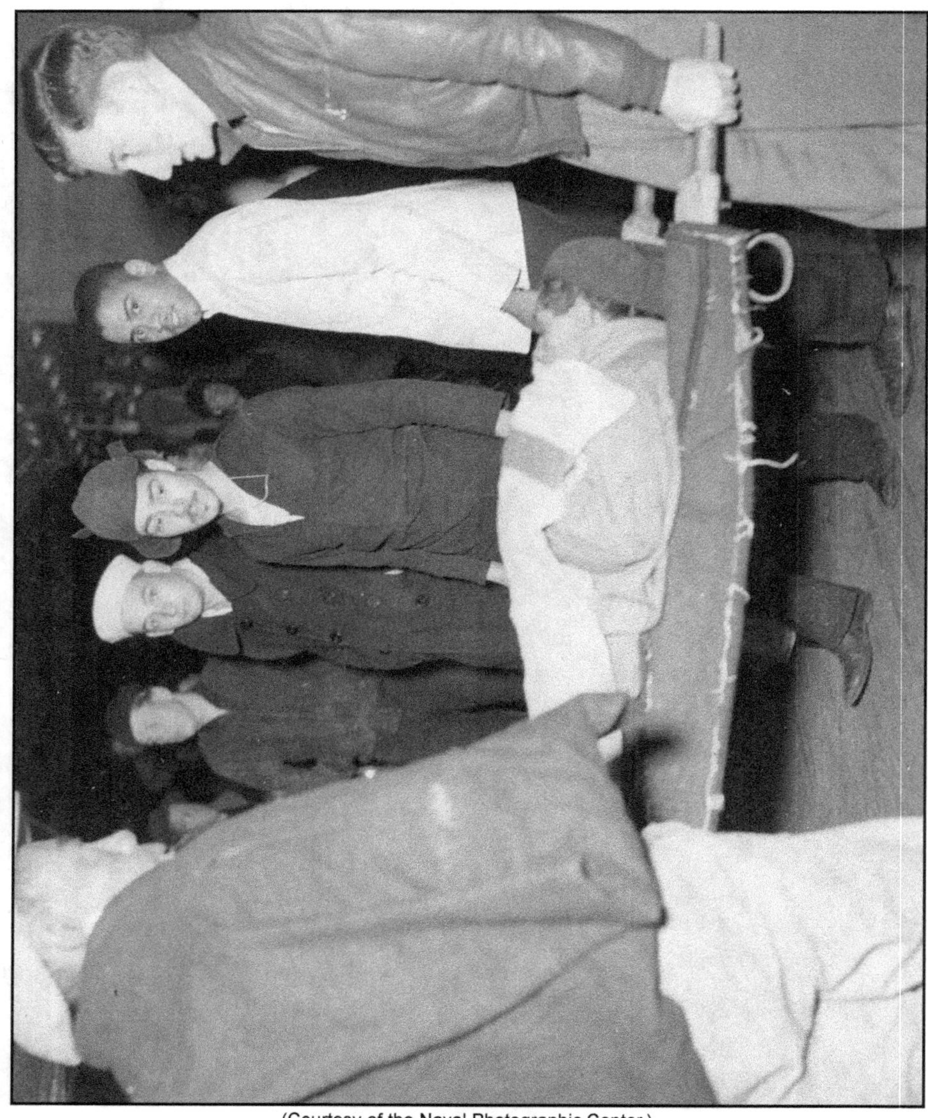

(Courtesy of the Naval Photographic Center.)

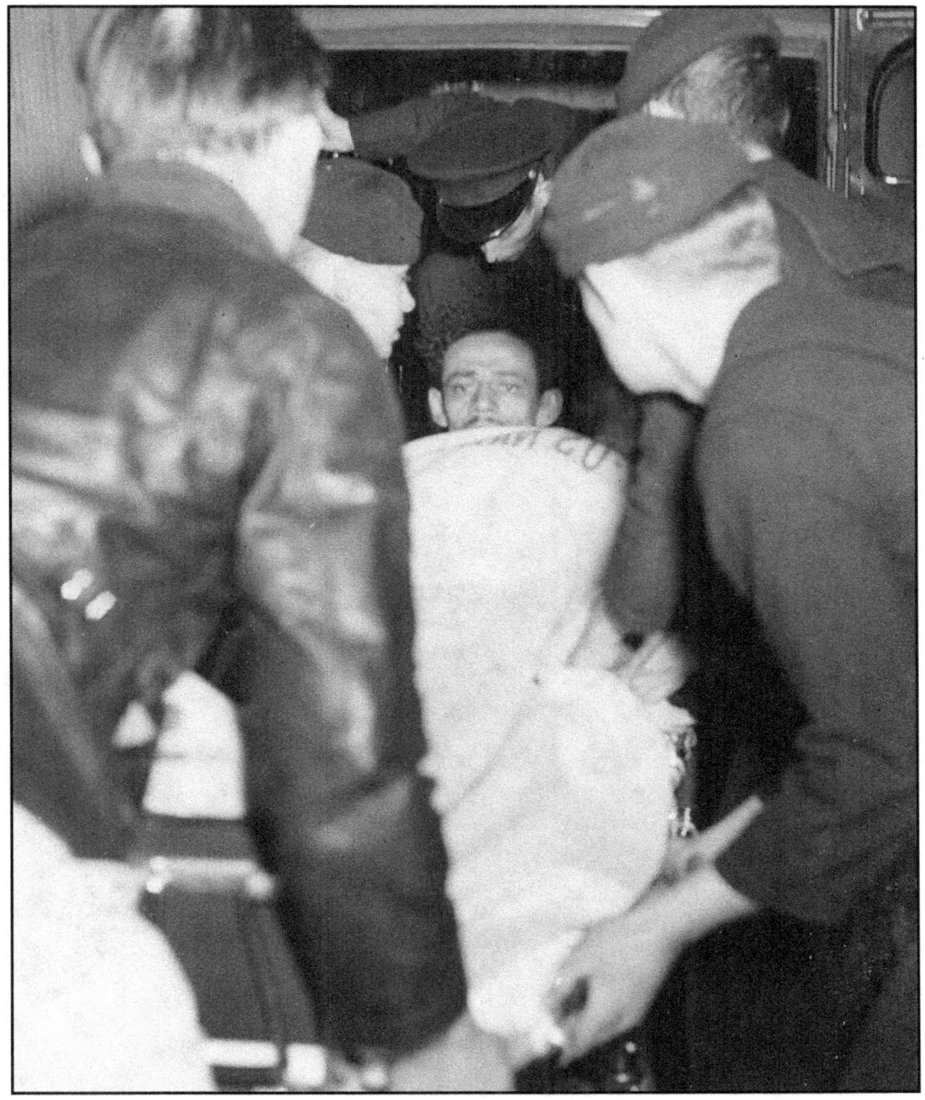

(Courtesy of the Naval Photographic Center.)

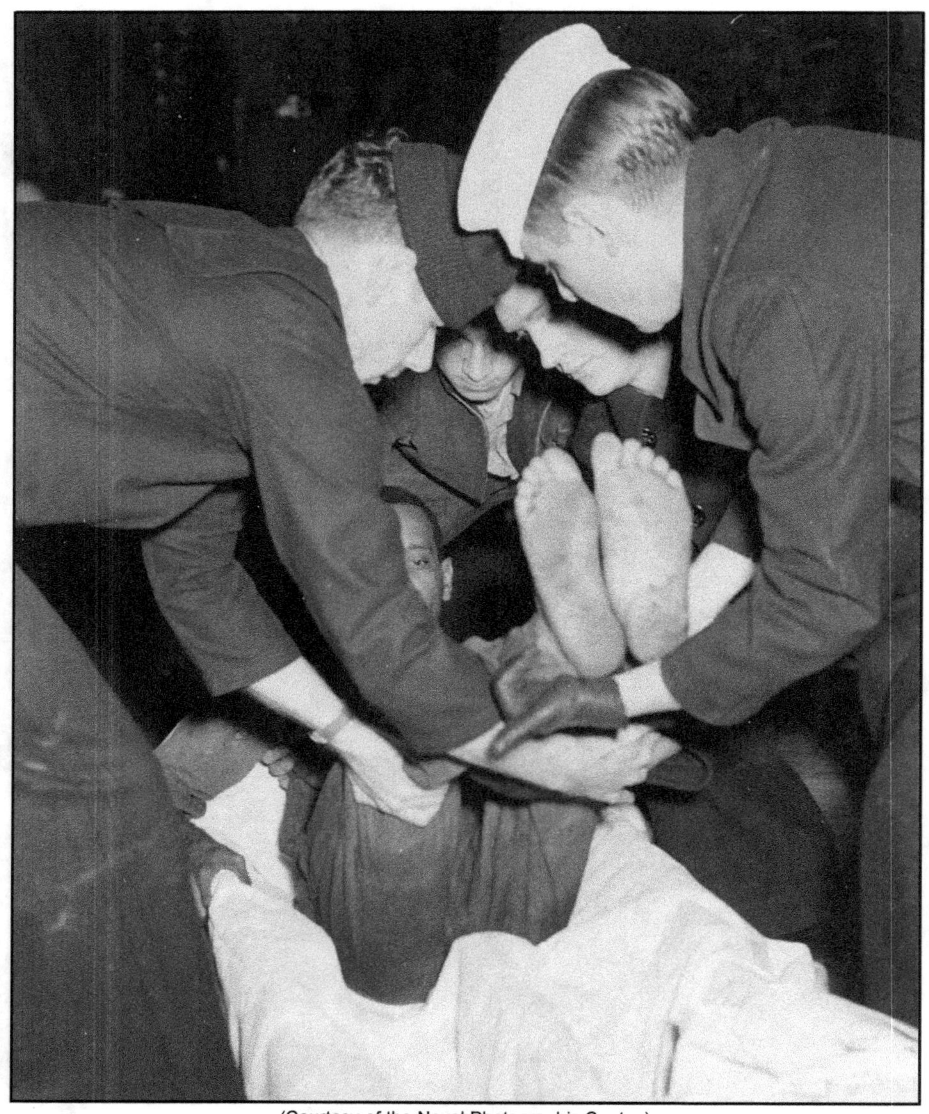

(Courtesy of the Naval Photographic Center.)

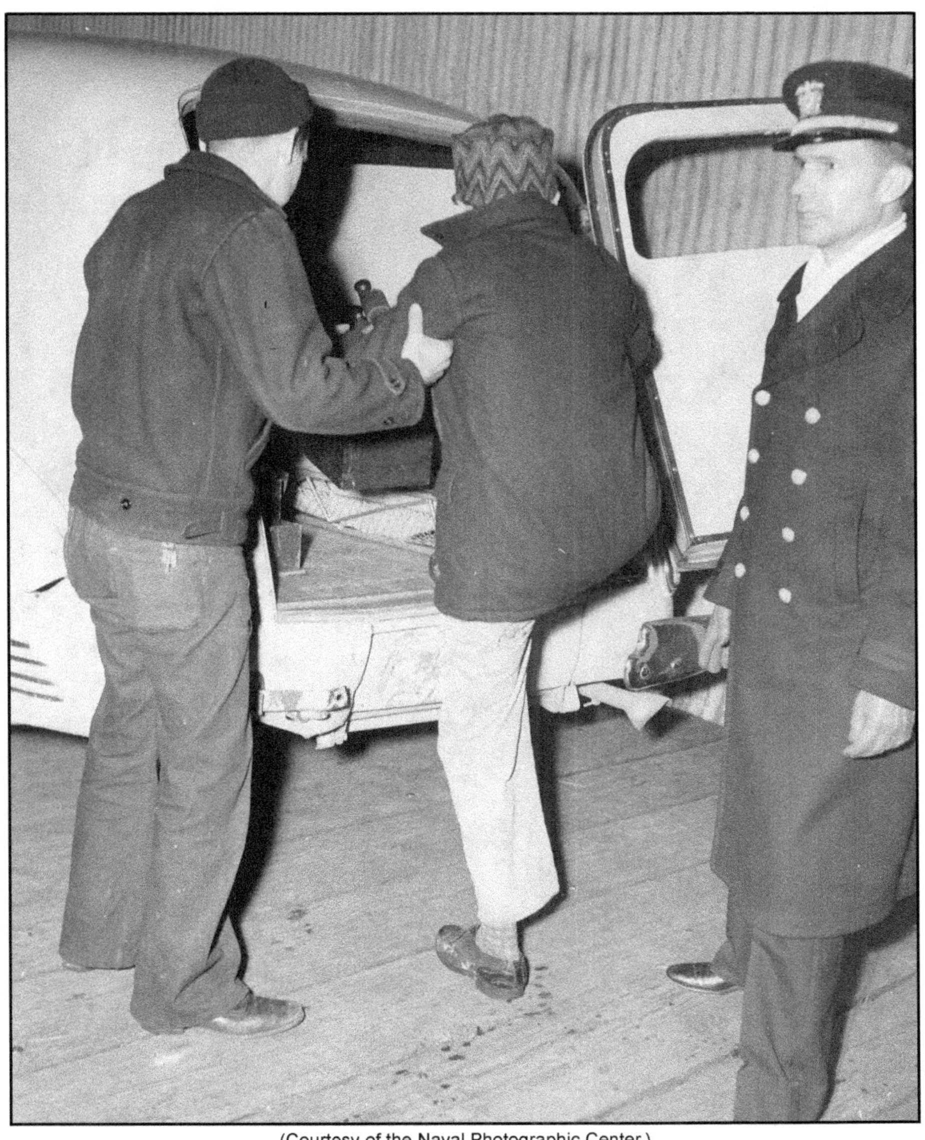

(Courtesy of the Naval Photographic Center.)

(Courtesy of the Naval Photographic Center.)

(Courtesy of the National Archives.)

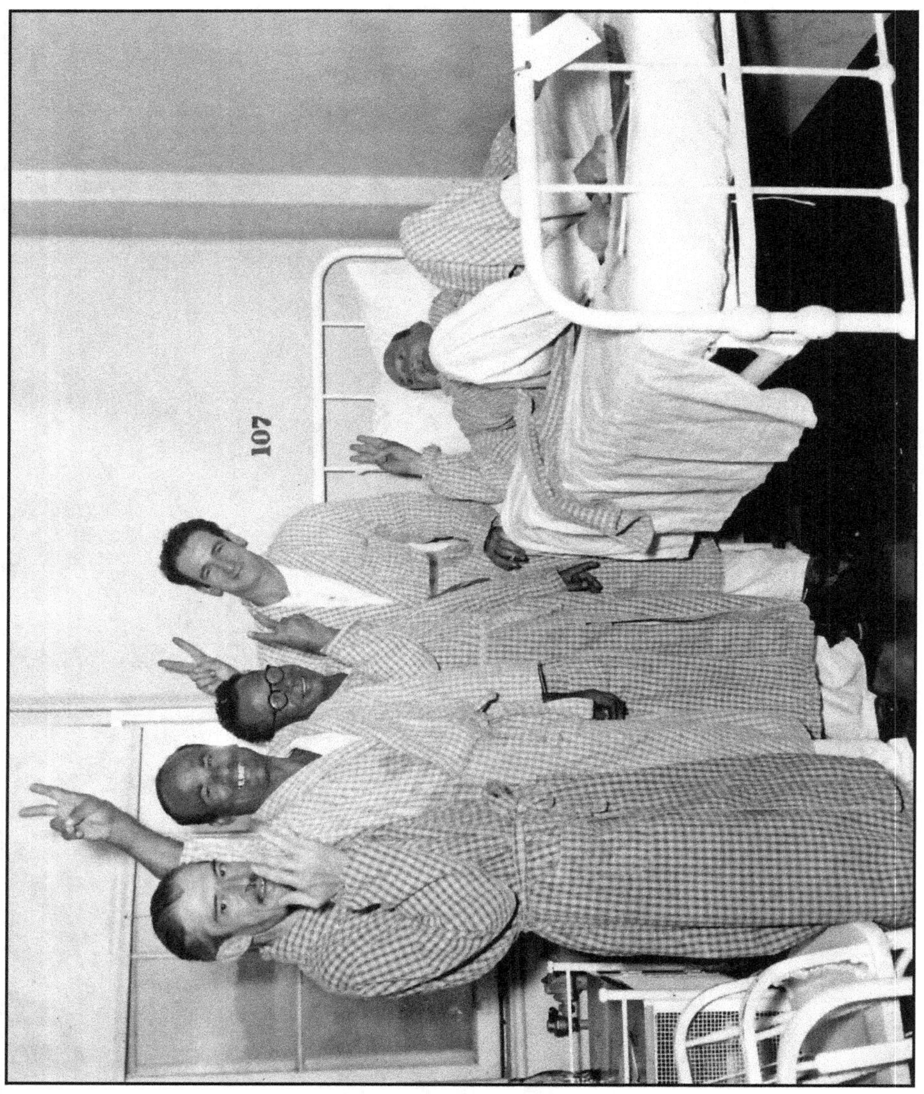

(From the author's collection.)

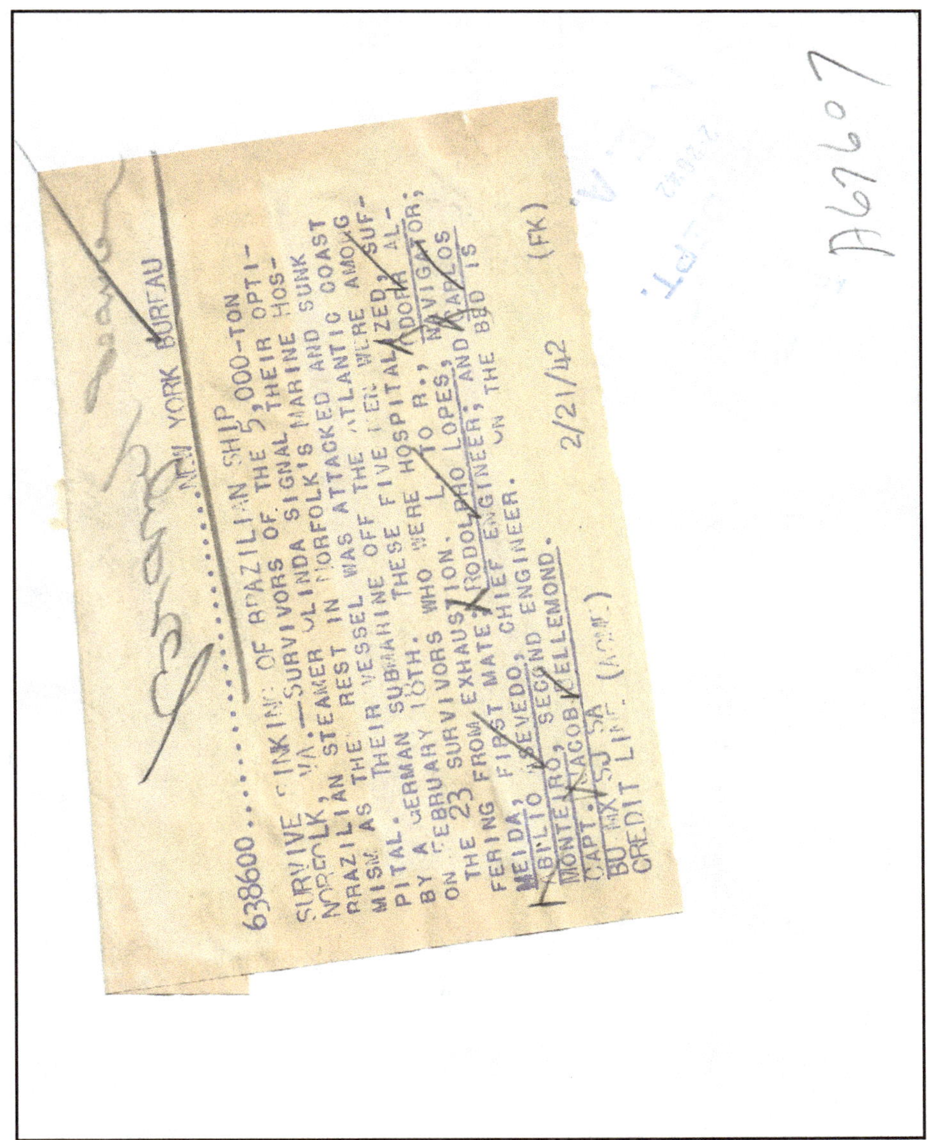

638600 ....NEW YORK BUREAU

SURVIVE SINKING OF BRAZILIAN SHIP

NORFOLK, VA.—SURVIVORS OF THE 5,000-TON BRAZILIAN STEAMER OLINDA SIGNAL THEIR OPTIMISM AS THEY REST IN NORFOLK'S MARINE HOSPITAL. THEIR VESSEL WAS ATTACKED AND SUNK BY A GERMAN SUBMARINE OFF THE ATLANTIC COAST ON FEBRUARY 18TH. THESE FIVE MEN WERE AMONG THE 23 SURVIVORS WHO WERE HOSPITALIZED, SUFFERING FROM EXHAUSTION. L. TO R., ODORIR ALMEIDA, FIRST MATE; RODOLPHO LOPES, NAVIGATOR; ABILIO ASEVEDO, CHIEF ENGINEER; AND CARLOS MONTEIRO, SECOND ENGINEER. ON THE BED IS CAPT. JACOB BELLEMOND.

2/21/42 (FK)

BU MX SJ SA

CREDIT LINE (ACME)

A67607

This is the reverse side of the photographic print on the facing page. (From the author's collection.)

AMERICAN CARGO WAR RISK REINSURANCE EXCHANGE
ROOM 1609 - 99 JOHN STREET
NEW YORK

LOSS COMMITTEE BULLETIN

February 24, 1942

No. 551

"OLINDA" (Brazilian)

EAST COAST SOUTH AMERICA FOR NEW YORK

SAILED JANUARY 1942

APPORTIONMENT No. 6

OUR FILE No. 1081

By the above mentioned vessel, which is reported in the Press as having been sunk due to enemy action February 18th, 1942, according to information now in hand you are interested in cargo insured against war risk to the extent of your proportion of the following amounts:

Appleton & Cox, Inc.	$ 36,565.
Chubb & Son	189,760.
Fireman's Fund Insurance Company	100,399.
Home Insurance Company	62,750.
Insurance Company of North America	150,000.
Standard Marine Insurance Company	337,750.
Royal Insurance Company	8,000.
	$ 885,224.

NOTE- We are endeavoring to ascertain whether the vessel has actually been lost and, if so, whether as a result of war or marine perils. Meanwhile, Subscribers should advise promptly lines on cargo insured against war risk.

(Courtesy of Drew Maser.)

AMERICAN CARGO WAR RISK REINSURANCE EXCHANGE
ROOM 1609 - 99 JOHN STREET
NEW YORK

LOSS COMMITTEE BULLETIN

February 27, 1942

No. 562

"OLINDA" (Brazilian)

EAST COAST SOUTH AMERICA FOR NEW YORK

SAILED JANUARY 1942

APPORTIONMENT No. 6

OUR FILE NO. 1081

By the above mentioned vessel, which is reported in the Press as having been sunk due to enemy action February 18th, 1942, according to information now in hand you are interested in cargo insured against war risk to the extent of your proportion of the following amounts, instead of $885,224., as per Loss Bulletin No. 551:

Appleton & Cox, Inc.	$ 36,565.
Chubb & Son	189,760.
Fireman's Fund Insurance Company	100,399.
Home Insurance Company	62,750.
Insurance Company of North America	150,000.
Standard Marine Insurance Company	337,750.
Royal Insurance Company	8,000.
Providence Washington Insurance Co.	17,067.
Universal Insurance Company	12,567.
	$ 914,858.

NOTE - The Committee has confirmed that claims per this vessel can be considered as resulting from war perils.

(Courtesy of Drew Maser.)

1941-42 LLOYD'S REGISTER. STEAMERS & MOTORSHIPS. OL

No. in Book. / Official No. / Code Letters.	Steamer's Name. Material, Rig, &c. / Late Name if any. / Special Surveys. No. of Decks, &c.	Regist'd Tonnage. Gross. / Under deck. / Net.	Character. ✠ for Special Survey. Date of last Survey.	Port of Survey.	Equipment Letter	Date when tail shaft last seen.	Built. When	By Whom / Where	Owners.	Length.	Breadth.	Depth.	Port of Registry. / Flag.	Engines.
29694 DHSG	**Olga** Iron (exDuesternbrook) 1Dk2trB	584 496 331					1882	G.Howaldt Kiel	MathiesReed.K.G.	175·6 B40'	25·3	15·8	Hamburg German WB	C.2Cy.20"&37½"-27" 61N Gebr.Howaldt,Kiel
29695 209 SVNK	**Olga E. Embiricos** (exBellview-33) ssHul.No.3-4,35 ssSch.No.1-39 1Dk(Stl)&Shelter dk(Stl)	4677 4297 2794	✠100A1 Shelter dk withfreeboard 8,40 BS8,40 ✠LMC11,38 Fitted for oil fuel 1,22 F.P. above 150° F.	Bcl	z	CL 7,39	1922 1mo	JReadhead &Sons,Ld. SouthShields Lloyd'sA✠CP	C.E.Embiricos CellDBa128'uE28 DTa58'1010t	400·3 415·0(O.L.) f168'1080t FPT72tAPT153t	52·1	25·9	Andros Greek FK ptCem Coll BHto Sh dk 5 „ „ U „	T.3Cy.25½",44"&73"-48" 180lb 455N 3SB,9cf,GS190,HS7749 JReadhead&Sons,Ld.S.S
29696 DHSH	**Olga Siemers** Sub.Sig. 1Dk	3347 2534 1927					1923	Nordsee-werkeA.G. Emden	G.J.H.Siemers&Co.	332·7 P28'B87'F32'	46·6	20·6	Hamburg German WB	T.3Cy.24⅞",38 1/16"&62"-41 246N Ottensener Mch.G.m.b.H.Alto
29697 YTDE	**Olga Topić** (exTrevose-35) D.F. ssCff.No.3-2,31 ssSpt.No.2-39 1Dk(Stl)&Shelter dk(Stl)	4375 4131 2742	✠100A1 Shelter dk withfreeboard 5,40 BS4,41 ✠LMC7,39	Gen	y	CL 5,40	1918 5mo	JReadhead &Sons,Ld. South Shields Lloyd'sA✠CP	SlobodnaPlovidba TopićD.D.(Ant. Topić,Mgr.) CellDBa131'uE28' f175'1008t	400·2	52·1	25·2	Susak Yugoslav FK 6BHCem APT50t	T.3Cy.26",43"&71½"-48" 180lb 483N 3SB,9cf,GS177,HS7198 J.Readhead&SonsLd.S.S
29698 DKAX	**Olga Traber** (exVindeggen-39) 1Dk	3132 2841 1830					1921	Armstrong Whitworth&Co.Ld. Newcastle	W.Traber&Co.	329·9 P33'B97'F32'	46·9	23·3	Hamburg German WB	T.3Cy.23½",39"&65"-45" 288N ArmstrongWhitworth&Co.L
29699 142604 GLDF	**Oligarch** (exBritishLantern-37) ssPts.No.3-6,31 ssShl.No.2-39 Mchy.Aft 2Dks(Stl)&Web frames D.F. Longitudinal framing	6894 6297 4078	✠100A1 12,40 MS6,39 ✠LMC BS3,40 Carrying Petroleum in bulk Fitted for oil fuel 8,18 F.P. above 150° F.	Gls	a†	CL 6,38	1918 8mo	Workman, Clark&Co.Ld Belfast Lloyd'sA✠CP	TheAdmiralty CellDBu B35'107tDTf43'640t	430·1 P99'B33'F56' FPT164tAPT60t	57·0	33·0	London British FK 19BHptCem (14BHtoUdk 5 „2nd„)	T.3Cy.27½",45"&75"-54" 190lb 684N 3SB,12cf,GS237,HS9666 WorkmanClark&CoLdB
29700 384 IBOZ	**Olimpia** (exWrayCastle-32,exParis, exRickmerRickmers) ssN.Yk.No.2-28 D.F. 2Dks(Stl)	6040 5577 3795	— 11,33	Nwc	a†		1920 7mo	Rickmers Akt.Ges. Bremerhaven	A.Lauro	435·0 419·0 P57'B136'F47' CellDB367'1293t	55·6	29·2	Naples Italian FK 7BHAsp FPT100t	T.3Cy.29½",46 1/16"&75 9/16"-53⅝" 580N 3SB,9cf,GS180,HS8070 A.G."Weser,"Bremen
29701	**Olimpo** TwinSc OilEng.	790 — 553					1884	A&J.Inglis Glasgow	Cia.Argentina de Nav.Mihanovich Ltda.	286·1	34·2	12·1	Bns.Aires Argentine	Oil Engines 2S.C.SA 4Cy.16 5/16"-18⅞" 194N J&CGBolindersCoLdSk
29702 PUMO	**Olinda** (exKennemerland-34,exCara) ssAms.2ndNo.3-1,30 1Dk(Stl)&Spar dk(Stl) &deep framing	4053 3758 2521	✠ ... 3,35 ✠	Ams	x		1905 12mo	W.Hamilton&Co.Ld. PortGlasgow	Cia.Carbonifera RioGrandense CellDBa122'uE24	359·9 P81'B105'F31'25·0 f146'843tFPT127t	50·3	17·0	R.Janeiro Brazilian FK 6BHCem APT30t	T.3Cy.25",41"&67"-45" 364N 2SB,6pf,GS119,HS4906 D.Rowan&Co.Glasgow
29703 213401	— (exOlindaU.O.-32,exOlinda) OilEng Carrying oil in bulk 1Dk	419 — 267	Feb 18, 1942				1915	UnionIron WorksCo. SanFrancisco	UnionOilCo.of California	134·9	26·1	14·1	L.Angeles Utd.States WB	Oil Engines 4S.C.SA 4Cy.13"-18" 66N WesternMach.Co.L.An.
29704 DHSJ	**Oliva** D.F. Sub.Sig 2Dks	7885 7384 4874					1921	Bremer Vulkan Vegesack	Aktiengesellschaft fürSeeschiffahrt	468·8 P55'B102'F41'	58·3	32·7	Hamburg German WB	T.3Cy.32 3/16",52⅞"&86 3/16"-55 1/16" 550N BremerVulkan,Vegesack
29705 DHSI	— D.F. 1Dk	1308 1041 721					1922	Nüske&Co. Stettin	ArgoReederei RichardAdler&Co.	242·1 Q71'B108'F40'	37·0	14·0	Bremen German WB	T.3Cy.17¼",27½"&45 11/16"-27 108N A.Borsig,Berlin
29706 118639 MCXD	**Olive** 3Mst ssBel.2ndNo.3-1,32 ssDub.No.2-40 Well deck Mchy.Aft 1Dk(Irn) Cargo battens not fitted	328 241 122	✠100A1 6,40 MS6,40 ✠LMC BS3,41	Dub	f	CL 5,40	1907 9mo	J Fullerton &Co. Paisley Lloyd'sA✠CP	FrontierTownS.S. Co.Ld.(J.Fisher &Sons,Ld.Mgrs.)	142·5 24·3 Q80'B7'F25' BK6'	23·4	10·2	Newry British 3BHCem FPT43t	C.2Cy.15"&34"-24" 130lb 47RH 1SB,2pf,GS40,HS1300 RenfrewBros.&Co.Irvine
29707 148889 GLQC	**Olivebank** TwinSc OilEng. ssGls.No.3-3,39 1Dk(Stl)&Shelter dk(Stl-ws)	5154 4768 3117	✠100A1 withfreeboard 6,41 DBS3,41 ✠LMC3,39 Carrying vegetable oil in deep tank Carrying oil F.P. above 150° F. in Fore Peak	Sws	a†	CL 2,39	1926 2mo	Harland& Wolff,Ld. Glasgow Lloyd'sA✠CP	BankLine,Ld. (A.Weir&Co. Mgrs.) CellDB 357'1121tTanks between tunnels	420·4 435·0(O.L.) Q80'B7'F25'	53·9	26·5	Glasgow British FK 7BHptCem (Coll to Sh dk 6 „ 2nd „) 15'251tDTf	Oil Engines 4S.C.SA 12Cy.24 7/16"-37⅝" 717NH DB1100lb Harland&Wolff,Ld.Gls. 32'1067tFPT106tAPT182
29708 216512 WDDA	**Oliver Olson** (exSanPedro-37, exPointBonita) 1Dk Fitted for oil fuel	2235 1945 1360	✠ ... 11,28 ✠				1918 6mo	AlbinaEng &MachWrks Portland,Or.	Oliver J.Olson&Co.	289·0 P24'B144'F32'	44·1	19·0	S.Francisco Utd.States FK	T.3Cy.22½",37½"&60"-42" 313NH EllicottMachineCorp.Bal.
29709 6009 PGMN	**Olivia** D.F. E.S.D. OilEng. 1Dk,2nd dk clear of cargo tanks Longitudinal framing at bottom&at deck Mchy.Aft CruiserStern	6307 5540 3600	✠100A1 12,40 ✠LMC7,39 Carrying Petroleum in bulk	Bat	a†	CL	1939 7mo	Cantieri RiunitiDell'Adriatico Monfalcone Lloyd'sA✠CP	N.V.Curaçaosche Scheepv.Maats. CellDBuE61'87t	428·1 446·3(O.L.) P87'B47'F50 DTf25'259tFPT106tAPT56t	54·5	30·9	TheHague Dutch FK 16BHptCem ptAsp	Oil Engines 4S.C.SA 6Cy.25 9/16"-55½" 377NH DB180lb Cant.RiunitiDell'Adriatico
29710	**Oljaren** (exMartha-41) D.F. OilEng. Mchy.Aft 1Dk CruiserStern	547 425 247	✠100A1 11,40 ✠LMC8,39 Carrying Petroleum in bulk	Skm	i	OG 2,40	1939 8mo	Werf de Noord Alblasserdam Lloyd'sA✠CP	SwedishGovernment(Kungl.Marinförvaltningen)	180·3 189·0(O.L.) Q62'Trunk85'F33' FPT117t	27·8	10·7	Stockholm Swedish FK 9BH APT20t	Oil Engines 4S.C.SA 8Cy.11"-17½" 94NHP DB145lb Klöckner-Humboldt-DeutzA.G.Köln-Deutz
29711														

This page from the *Lloyd's Register* shows the *Olinda's* final listing. Note that she was not owned by Hapag at the time of her loss.

At first blush, the *Olinda* does not appear to have any relevance to the *U-111*. The vessels sank twenty years apart and were related to two different wars. It is the *existence* of the *Olinda* that is relevant, and the fact that the name was used to identify a location that is *not* the *Olinda*.

This begs the question: Where *is* the *Olinda*?

The earliest locations in English are found in archival documents that were generated during World War 2 by the Fifth Naval District, immediately after the sinking and the rescue of survivors. These documents are not available to stubborn Internet-only researchers because they are stored loose in National Archives boxes as individual sheets of paper.

One of these primary documents gave the position of the burning vessel as 37-30N and 74-00W (pronounced 37 degrees and thirty minutes north latitude, and seventy-four degrees west longitude).

Another document gave the position as 37-30N and 75-00W. The difference between these two positions is sixty nautical miles from east and west.

A third document gave three different positions on the same sheet of paper: 37-38N / 74-00W, 37-55N / 74-00W, and 37-30 N / 75 W. The difference between these three positions is sixty nautical miles from east to west, and seventeen nautical miles from north to south. Keep in mind that these positions were approximated by aircraft. This sheet of paper also gave positions for two locations where survivors in lifeboats were picked up by the U.S. destroyer *Dallas*.

The rescue positions of the two lifeboats were 37-40 N / 74-13 W and 37-40 N / 74-23 W.

Among official publications that were printed for distribution, the earliest one that gave the location of the sunken *Olinda* is found in a confidential document called "Ships sunk or attacked by enemy submarines within the Sea Frontiers of the U. S. from Jan.1, 1942 to Mar. 31, 1943 (inclusive)" That location was 37-30N / 75-00W.

This same location was given in the undated but contemporary Appendix "A" of the "List of attacks by the enemy in waters of the Fifth Naval district."

As published in the *Wreck Information List* of 1945, the *Olinda* was listed as Wreck No. 256. This list was compiled by all data that were currently obtainable by the U.S. Hydrographic Office. The latitude and longitude were given as 37-55-00 / 74-00-00, Any location number with that many zeroes is immediately suspect; the position is far too general to possess any degree of accuracy. The depth was given as 101 fathoms, or 606 feet. A wreck symbol has been placed at that location on the U.S. Coast and Geodetic Survey chart.

This information was repeated in the *Navy Wreck List* of 1957.

In the Second Edition of the Confidential report that is called the *Non-Submarine Contacts* list of 1968, which includes the Western Atlantic and Caribbean Sea, the *Olinda* wreck number is 0394, which repeats the position that is given in the *Wreck Information List*.

Coincidentally, the 1979 third edition of *Non-Submarine Contacts* mentions the *U-111*. Not the World War 1 *U-111*; the World War 2 *U-111*, which was sunk in combat off the Canary Islands. It also mentions the *U-2513*, the U-boat that I helped to discover.

The 1989 edition of *Lloyd's War Losses* claimed that the *Olinda* sank at "37 30 N., 75 W.", which is sixty miles westward of the previous positions, and some thirty to thirty-five miles east of Parramore Island, Virginia.

In 1992, when Loran-C was available for locating shipwrecks off the eastern seaboard, commercial anglers placed the *Olinda* at 26710.2 / 42121.5. This position corresponds with the location that was given in the *Wreck Information List*. These coordinates are the ones that I used in the Loran lists of *Shipwrecks of Delaware and Maryland* (1990) and *Shipwrecks of Virginia* (1992).

In 2018, dive boat skipper Ted Green provided me with a new set of coordinates that he obtained from a commercial fishing friend of his. These numbers, in Global Position System format, which mimics latitude and longitude, are 37-47.268 / 74-11.873.

Later, Ted Green gave these numbers to Joe Mazraani.

As noted above, in addition to being a charter boat skipper who owned and operated a dive shop in Salisbury, Maryland, Ted Green was also an experienced deep-water mixed-gas diver and rebreather diver; plus he was a technical diving instructor as well as a technical diving instructor trainer. By 2018, he was changing his lifestyle and was no longer interested in utilizing his skills to dive on a wreck at a depth of 390 feet: the approximate depth of the *Olinda* wreck according to his fishing friend.

Wreck-divers are always on the lookout for unknown shipwrecks to explore. In 1989, when I first researched the *U-111* and the *Olinda*, there were no technical wreck-divers who were diving on deep shipwrecks that were located at depths where helium mixes were required. Technical wreck-diving, as differentiated from recreational diving, commenced in 1990, with Billy Deans in Florida and with Ken Clayton, Pete Manchee, and this author on the *Ostfriesland*. With the expansion of technical diving in the following years, more and more divers sought shipwrecks that lay at depths that were previously considered to be inaccessible.

In 2020, the *Olinda* became one of those unknown shipwrecks. And because Ted Green was willing to share the GPS numbers, interest in the *Olinda* waxed among technical divers.

To add confirmation to Ted Green's "numbers," as position coordinates are called, Ben Roberts found an almost identical position on the AWOIS list. (AWOIS is the acronym for Automated Wreck and Obstruction Information System.) Those numbers were 37/47/29.75 and 74/12/03.51. The numbers were translated from Loran C to the Coast Guard system of writing GPS numbers.

The purpose of this lengthy exercise is to educate my readers about

RECRD	993	VESSLTERMS	UNKNOWN	CHART	12200	AREA	D
		CARTOCODE	0999	SNDINGCODE		DEPTH	0

NATIVLAT	37/47/29.28	NATIVLON	074/12/05.01	NATIVDATUM	6
LAT83	37/47/29.75	LONG83	074/12/03.51	GPQUALITY	Low
LATDEC	37.791597222222	LONDEC	74.200975	GPSOURCE	NA

History
00993
DESCRIPTION
18 IN 62-65 FATHOMS, HUNG BY TRAWL FISHERMAN, NAD27 GP CONVERTED FROM LORAN C,
OBSERVED RATES;9960X-26760.8MS,9960Y-42025.0MS(APPROX. 1979)

SURVEY REQUIREMENTS
NOT DETERMINED

REFERENCE:		YEARSUNK		SYSTEMNUM	966

the challenges that are presented to wreck-divers who are actively seeking to locate and identify shipwrecks.

To expand the lesson that I noted above, my readers must understand that U-boats kept precise records of their location as they prowled the ocean in search of Allied targets. The importance of maintaining exact positions was not so that future historians could use them to identify newly found shipwrecks, but so that U-boats did not stray into another U-boat's territory, and accidentally torpedo a fellow Nazi submarine. Not only did U-boat skippers log their traveling locations, but they radioed their locations to U-boat Headquarters. This enabled U-boat headquarters to direct U-boats to or away from specific areas.

German Sources

In 1968, Jurgen Rohwer published *Die U-Boot-Erfolge Der Achsenmachte 1939-1945.* Fifteen years later, in 1983, an English translation was published as *Axis Submarine Successes 1939 – 1945.* This book quickly became the bible for shipwreck researchers, not only because it incorporated the work of the Allied Assessors in assigning the names of vessels that were sunk by specifically numbered U-boats, but because it provided the location at which the attacks occurred.

Rohwer noted that the *U-432* (Kapitanleutnant Heinz-Otto Schultze) shelled and torpedoed the neutral vessel *Olinda* on February 18, 1942, at 37-30 N / 75. W. The advantage of Rohwer's list was that, as director of the Bibliothek fur Zeitgeschichte (Library of Contemporary History), he had access to German records and U-boat KTB's (kriegstagebuch), or deck logs. Yet that position in latitude and longitude is nowhere near the position that Rohwer gave for the position in accordance with the German grid system, which was given as CA 5817.

In the grid system, U-boat skippers referred to a grid chart by recording a position in a large, lettered grid square, then located the position on nine two-numbered squares within the lettered grid square, then recorded the location on one of the nine two-numbered zero-ending squares within that square, and finalized the position on one of the

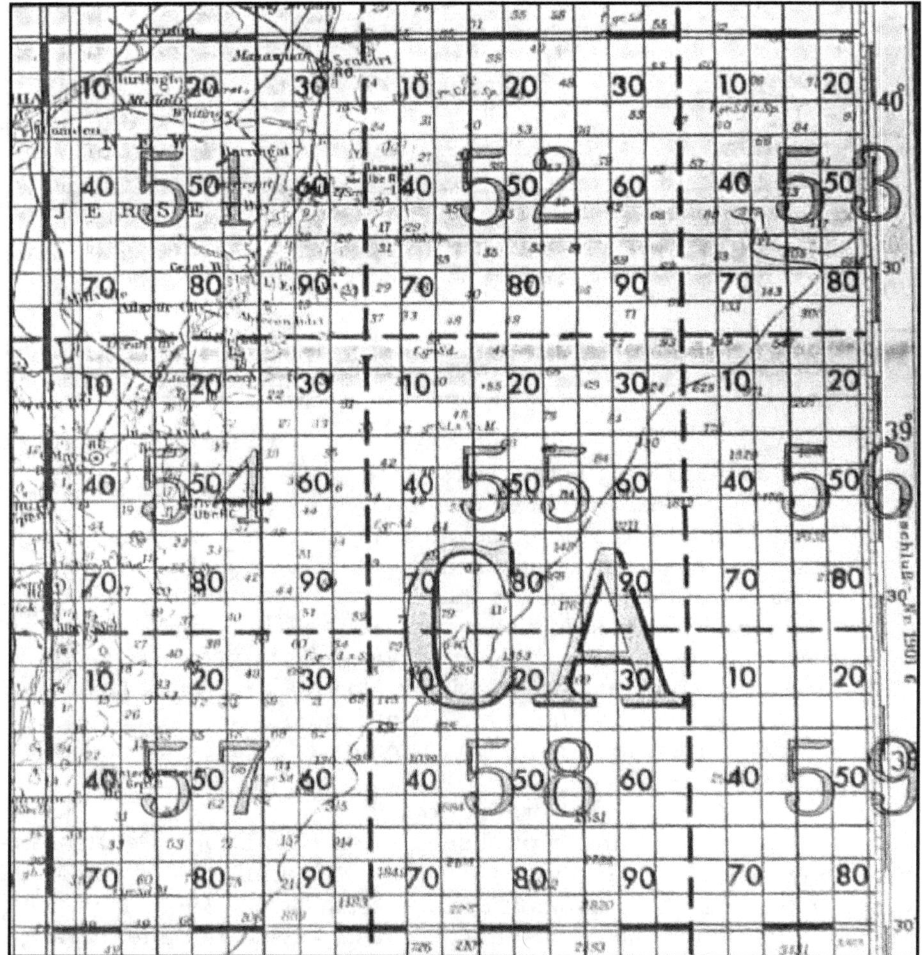

single-numbered squares which took the place of the concluding zero.

The lettered grid square off the U. S. eastern seaboard, between Rhode Island and Georgia, was designated as CA. Within CA lay the numbered square in which an event occurred, in this case 58, which designated the ocean offshore of Delaware, Maryland, and Virginia. Within grid square 58 lay the number 10, and within number 10 lay the smallest square, which had the single digit square that converted the zero in the 10 to a 7, thus yielding 17.

To recapitulate in different words, within grid square CA, Schultze located grid square 58, within which he located grid square 10, within which he located grid square 7, so that 10 became 17.

This coded grid system did not lead to pinpoint accuracy, nor was it intended to. But it was close enough to enable U-boat Command to ascertain where every U-boat was located whenever it checked in with headquarters.

When CA 5817 is translated to latitude and longitude, it yields 38-15 N / 73-58 W. Thus the two positions in Rohwer's books contradict each other, each position being different from the other.

To add confusion, the grid number in Schultze's deck log is not CA 5817, as in Rohwer's book, but CA 5841. Perhaps CA 5817 was a typographical error, but that seems unlikely under the circumstances: the circumstances being that Rohwer's book seems not to have used Schultze's deck log but instead copied the location from "Ships sunk

Datum und Uhrzeit	[illegible]	Vorkommnisse
		diesen Entschluß der Kapitän durch Zeichen klar. Er hat offebar nichts anderes erwartet und ist damit ganz einverstanden. Er bedankt sich vielmals für die nachsichtige Behandlung und geht erleichtert von Bord.
[illegible]100	CA. 5841 4[illegible] BRT	[illegible]ngschuß aus Rohr I. Treffer mittschiffs nach 52 Sek. (Tiefe 3 m) Anschließend mit Artillerie nach ca. 40 Treffern ~~xxxx~~ in die Wasserlinie und Aufbauten. Schiff sinkt langsam tiefer und fängt in der Mitte zu brennen an.
2120 2145		Flugzeug im N an der Kimm entdeckt dann offenbar den brennenden Dampfer und dreht zu. Alarm. Auf 30 m unter Wasser abgelaufen.
2210		Auf Sehrohrtiefe. Flugzeug sehr nah anfliegend. Wieder auf 30 m. Sinken des Schiffes sehr laut im Horchgerät beobachtet. Auf Sehrohrtiefe. Flugzeug kreist immer noch. Der selbe Typ wie am Vormittag. Ähnlich wi[illegible] unserer Kondor.
		Von "Olinda" nichts mehr zu sehen. Sicherheitshalber laufe ich noch einmal unter Wasser zurück und treffe auch 2324 Uhr di[e] beiden verlassenen Flöße. Das Schiff ist weg.
2300	Ostk. USA. CA. 5841	
2320 2430		Starke Rauchfahne in 65 Grad. Wandert langsam bis 35 Grad. Nach dem Abfliegen der feindliche Maschine aufgetaucht und verfolgt. Peilung 30 Grad. In der Dämmerung geht die Fühlung verloren.
19.2. 0138		Getaucht zum Horchen. Keine Peilung.
0157		Aufgetaucht. ~~Auf N-Kurs (nach New York)~~ nachgestoßen.
0300	Ostk. USA. CA. 5581 ~~NW 2, 2, 0, 1022~~ + 7 Grad	
0320		Rauchfahne 340 Grad. E = ca. 8 sm. Gegner fährt abgeblendet. Kurs um 355 Grad. Fahrt 10,5 sm.
0618		Doppelschuß aus Rohr I u. III (Tiefe 3 [illegible] E = 1500, Vg. 11 sm, Lage 70 Grad)
0620	CA. 5288 4000 BRT	2 Treffer vorn 20 und Mitte (Laufzeit 75 = 1125 m) Nachdem sich Qualm und Rauch v[er]zogen haben sind vom Schiff nur noch ein Ölfleck und Wrackträmmer übrig geblieben. Mit Et. wurde nichts gegeben.

or attacked by enemy submarines within the Sea Frontiers of the U. S. from Jan.1, 1942 to Mar. 31, 1943 (inclusive).” That location was 37-30N and 75-00W.” This makes me wonder why Rohwer would do such a thing when he had access to Schultze's deck log, from which he could have obtained the actual grid square code (which he then misinterpreted).

The long and short of this bewildering array of egregious errors implies that Rohwer's book is unreliable, at least in this particular instance.

Shultze's actual grid system code number translates roughly to 38-15 N / 73-45 W. At that location on the nautical chart, the depth of water is 62 fathoms, or 372 feet. It is almost impossible to believe that Shultze did not know his location when he sank the *Olinda*. I cannot imagine a situation in which a U-boat skipper was off course by fifty-one nautical miles: this being the distance between Shultze's grid number and the location of the wreck that Ben Roberts side-scanned and tentatively identified as the *Olinda*. (See below.) With regard to this newly found shipwreck, Schultze's position differs in both latitude and longitude. Yet there it is.

Admiral Karl Doenitz, head of the Nazi U-boat division, invented wolf pack tactics: a system in which a U-boat communicated the location of an Allied convoy to headquarters, which then communicated that location to nearby U-boats so that they could home in on the convoy, surround it like Amerindians whooping around a wagon train, then attack in concert from various directions.

There is no truth to the rumor that hard-core East Coast wreck divers commonly refer to Admiral Karl Doenitz as Dunkin' Doenitz, even though he is personally responsible for all the U-boat-caused casualties that have occurred off the eastern seaboard. (From the author's collection.)

Thus it was vitally important for every U-boat to know precisely where it was located at all times, and for U-boat headquarters maintain that information among all the U-boats that were at sea. This is why U-boat deck logs can be indispensable for locating shipwrecks.

Researchers should know that the National Archives' remote building in College Park, Maryland has microfilms of most U-boats that returned from their patrols.

In the case of the *Olinda*, all this research of aggregating "numbers" did not necessarily establish the location of the wreck. Instead, much of the research established where the *Olinda* was *not* located. It was *not* located at the site that commercial anglers called the *Olinda* wreck. A shipwreck was there, but it was not the *Olinda*. In Ben Roberts' eyes, this kind of negative information - that the wreck at that location was a submarine - helped to strengthen my declaration that the *Olinda* wreck was the *U-111*.

Meanwhile, Ben Roberts was deeply embroiled in his planned summer occupation of side-scanning selected shipwrecks from Massachusetts to Virginia. As already noted, this massive project enabled him to create and collect side-scan sonar images of an additional 191 wreck sites in 2021. Wow!

Also recall that, unfortunately, in his words, "The *U-111* was excluded because the consensus at the time was that it rested in waters too deep (˜1,600') for my equipment – and I was not yet convinced by Gentile's theory that the *Olinda* wreck nearby (thought to be the sub *R-8* but was actually *U-111*) had been misidentified."

But all wasn't lost. In deep water off the coast of Virginia . . . but let Ben Roberts tell the story in his own words from his Facebook post:

"Being one of only a few large ships yet to be located in the region, *Olinda* was a natural search focus for the first phase of our 2021 Offshore Wrecks Survey. German war records placed the sinking location deep in Baltimore Canyon, so we contacted UNC-Wilmington professor Dr. Steve Ross, who together with URI professor Dr. Rod Mather had conducted a multibeam sonar survey of the canyon in 2011. After confirming that the wreck was not located during Ross and Mather's expedition, we consulted with ESS collaborators Rusty Cassway, Gary Gentile and Michael Barnette. The team found a consistent pattern in the German records that seemed to invalidate the official sinking location in Baltimore Canyon, and suggested a new search area many miles away. Within the new search area, our machine learning / artificial intelligence algorithms had identified a search prospect from our database of commercial fishing 'hangs' (underwater obstructions that snag nets and other gear) that appeared worthy of surveying. We passed directly over the wreck almost immediately after arriving on-site on Wednesday, necessitating evasive action to avoid striking the wreck with our towed sonar gear and potentially damaging or losing it in the wreckage.

"Thus, it was the combination of collaborative efforts, multiple perspectives and the application of various techniques – some based in historical research, others more technological – that directly produced the discovery.

"Today *Olinda* is upright and in mostly-intact condition with as much as 35' of relief above the bottom. Her bow is well-preserved, with the windlass and anchor chains visible atop the foc'sle. Some of her cargo holds are intact while others are more deteriorated, and her midship superstructure appears to be in a moderate state of collapse. Her stern is severely deteriorated and seemingly shortened, possibly from impacting the bottom when she sunk, and/or portions of it sank elsewhere. At a depth of 330', the wreck lies just within reach of the most qualified technical divers, and an expedition is currently being planned to obtain photos and video footage of the site to further document it."

The date of Roberts' discovery of the *Olinda* was June 2, 2021.

Here is another example of Ben Roberts' instrumental method of matching an historical photograph of a vessel - in this case the *Olinda* as the *Kennemerland* - with his side-scan sonar image of the shipwreck on the bottom.

I hate to take a dissenting point of view, especially after the exuberance of locating and then diving on an unknown shipwreck, but an important part of wreck-diving and discovery is authenticating a wreck's identity.

The first divers on the wreck of the presumed *Olinda* were Jon Haws, Richie Kohler, Pat McLaughlin, and Jason Speiser. All four breathed mixed gas from a rebreather. For a thirty-minute bottom time they spent three and a half hours decompressing. Ugh! But the ambient visibility was clear – even awesome, considering the depth of 330 feet.

One highlight of the dive was the recovery of a bell by Richie Kohler. Unfortunately, the bell did not have the name of the vessel engraved on it. Drat! Another highlight was the recovery of the helm stand by Jon Haws. The top of the stand had the manufacturer's name stamped on it, so this may eventually lead to the identity of the vessel. Yet another highlight was the recovery of ten items of china. Some of the china items were stamped with the shipping line company HAPAG. This was bad news.

After extensive research, I found no correlation between the *Olinda* and the Hamburg-Amerikanische Packetfahrt-Aktien-Gesellschaft (better known as the Hamburg American Line, or HAPAG). The *Lloyd's Register* proves that the *Olinda* was never owned by HAPAG nor by any subsidiary of HAPAG.

The *Olinda's* original name was *Cara*. She was built in 1905 by William Hamilton & Company in Port Glascow, Scotland. Her first owner was the Cara Steam Ship Company, of Liverpool, England.

In 1913, the *Cara* was sold to Koninklijke Hollandsche Lloyd (Royal Holland Lloyd), of Amsterdam, the Netherlands, and was renamed *Kennemerland*.

In 1934, the *Kennemerland* was sold to Cia Carbonifer Rio Grandense, in Rio de Janeiro, Brazil, and was renamed *Olinda*. She was operating under that name and ownership at the time of her loss.

What did this contradictory information mean? It normally meant that the shipwreck that Ben Roberts side-scanned was *not* the *Olinda*. Yet I do not like to jump to conclusions. Stranger things have happened in shipwreck discoveries and research.

Take the *Montgomery*, for example. Before the wreck was tentatively identified as the *Montgomery*, Harold Moyers recovered a brass key with a tag on which the name "SS *Dallas*" was engraved. Yet there was no vessel by that name anywhere in the registries of the period.

A bell with the name *Balaena* engraved on it was found by Joel Entler on an old sailing vessel in the Mud Hole off Manasquan, New Jersey. Again, no such name appeared in contemporary registries. So despite having the name in bronze, no correlation was ever found between the shipwreck and the name on the bell. The true name of the wreck is still unknown.

On the other hand, as I showed above, the deck log of the *U-432* claimed that it sank the *Olinda* fifty-one miles northeast of the place where Ben Roberts side-scanned the wreck to which he has given the name *Olinda*. Shipwreck research is much like a mystery novel, except that you don't always learn who-done-it; or you might have to wait years and years before the truth presents itself.

In the case of the *Olinda*, I have questions for which I do not presently have answers. So, it's back to the archives and back under water. In summation, let's compare our differences. Keep in mind that we are not arguing or fighting: we are *debating*.

Ben told me that he used uboat.net to obtain the position of the *Olinda*. I never thought of checking uboat.net because it was a secondary source, whereas I rely on primary sources. As soon as I checked uboat.net for vessels that the *U-432* was given credit for sinking, and linked to the *Olinda*, I spotted two errors: the locations (both grid code and lat/lon) were the same as those in Rohwer, leading me to presume that *Axis Submarine Successes 1939 - 1945* was the source.

For Ben's purposes, this positional error did not necessarily invalidate the usefulness of the data if they were used to create a pattern. "That's about 42 nautical miles northeast of the actual wreck site. I also recall that we compared the actual and logged positions for a few vessels sunk just before (or after) *Olinda* and found similar offsets, kind of like the exercise you [meaning this author] did for the Black Sunday wrecks off NJ. For *Olinda*, the offsets didn't form a perfect pattern, but it was good enough to indicate that the wreck could easily be *Olinda*."

Ben found, "the *U-432's* position for the *Buarque* sinking on 2/15/1942 is off by 13.3 nautical miles, at a heading (from the logged position to the wreck) of 6 degrees true. The *Olinda* (2/18/1942) is off by 41.6 miles @ 224 degrees. The *Miraflores* (2/19) is off by 40.2 miles @ 224 degrees.

(See the *Buarque* entry in *Shipwrecks of North Carolina: North.* See the *Miraflores* chapter in *Shipwreck Sagas*.)

"This would seem to suggest that something happened in the three days between when the *Buarque* was sunk and when the *Olinda* was sunk that caused a significant amount of navigational error, such as having to resort to dead reckoning due to inability to take a noon sighting due to weather, running submerged, etc. The fact that the position errors (~40 miles @ 224 degrees) are virtually identical for *Olinda* and *Miraflores* is striking, and this seems unlikely to be coincidental."

Ben further noted, "In my opinion, the rectangular portholes, manufacturing location of Glasgow for the helm stand, vessel size / type / apparent age, and the presence of what appeared to be vats in the cargo holds are all additional supporting evidence for *Olinda* as the wreck's identity. But considering everything together, I'm personally confident (90%+) that the wreck is probably *Olinda*."

I can find no flaws in these arguments. The evidence, while not overwhelming, is certainly indicative of Roberts' conclusion. In fact, I will go so far as to grant that I *want* the wreck to be the *Olinda*. I am partly swayed by the side-scan sonar image that looks so much like the *Olinda*. But because looks can be deceiving, I am cautious of being quite so accepting of his confidence. After all, most freighters from the pre-War era possessed the same general hull design and appearance. After a wreck has collapsed due to natural deterioration, the layout of the superstructure is generally indecipherable.

I would gladly concede the argument if the contrary evidence were not so persuasive.

First and foremost is Schultze's deck-log position (not Rohwer's), which is fifty-one miles away from the wreck site. Then there is the written report in the deck log. Here is a rough translation that is based on an Internet German-to-English application:

"The decision of the captain [of the *Olinda*] made clear by signs. Apparently he didn't expect anything else and is quite happy with that. [Schultze released the *Olinda's* captain instead of keeping him prisoner.] He's dunking [illegible word] the indulgent treatment and is relieved to disembark.

"Catch boost from Rohr I. Hit midships after 52 sec. Depth 3 m[eters]. Then with artillery after approx. 40 hits in the water line and Saute [?]. Ship sinks deeper and starts to break in the middle.

"Airplane approaching very close. Again at 30 m. Sinking of the ship very loudly in the listening device Boobservet [?]. At periscope depth. Plane is still circling. The same guy as before. Similar to our Kandor. [The Focke-Wulf Condor was a four-engine German aircraft.]

"Nothing more to be seen of *Olinda*. To be on the safe side, I walk back under water and at 11:24 p.m. I meet the two deserted float [?]. The ship is gone. [By "float" I think that Schultze or the translater meant lifeboats or life rafts.]

"Heavy plume of smoke at 65 degrees. Hikes slowly to 35 degrees. Appeared and pursued after enemy machine took off. Metric 30 degrees. In the twilight the light is lost.

"Dipped to listen. No polarization. Surfaced. Followed up on course N (towards New York)."

Although the side-scan sonar image did not show a large break in the hull, it did show a crack amidships on the starboard side. It also showed that the stern was either missing or broken down into a debris field.

Yet, some additional evidence that bolsters Roberts' contention is that the USS *Dallas* found the lifeboats in the vicinity of the wreck site that Roberts found. Plus, the positions that were estimated by the officers of the *Olinda* were not located as far north as the position that was given in the deck log of the *U-432*.

An unidentified shipwreck was much like a real-life crime scene: almost never was every piece of evidence accounted for. Except in mystery novels, there were always pieces that did not fit into the puzzle, and were never resolved satisfactorily.

Ben Roberts' arguments were persuasive. My primary argument was faith in the capability of U-boat skippers to calculate their positions. For me to accept Roberts' argument in place of my own, meant that I must recant my faith in Nazi infallibility, and acknowledge that *U-432* appeared to have been lost. This was like a child admitting that there was no Santa Klaus.

Then there is my very own dictum, which I have said and written numerous times: "Most shipwrecks are identified not by the recovery of an item that bears the name of the wreck, but by a preponderance of evidence." In this case, the preponderance of evidence was with Roberts; all I had was my faith in the ability of U-boat captains to know where they were. I won't go as far as to state that Roberts' deduction is definitely correct, but I will concede that the scales of justice tipped in his favor, despite the existence of HAPAG china on a vessel that never had any connection with that shipping line.

Hopefully, additional dives will eventually deliver the absolute truth.

I had hoped that in the 2021 diving season, a trip could be organized to explore the *U-111*: not necessarily by diving on the wreck, but by some remote means. As a way to maintain what I perceived to be foundering interest in the *U-111*, on July 21, 2021, I sent an email to Rusty Cassway in which I again provided him with Ted Green's GPS coordinates of the *Olinda* wreck, and told him to compare them with the lat/lon that I had published for the *U-111*. He had already done so, but nonetheless the year slipped away as if the *U-111* had been placed on his back burner. Perhaps it was not even simmering. Even without a vote of confidence from Roberts and Cassway, I maintained confidence that the submarine at the *Olinda* wreck site was the *U-111*.

From: gary@ggentile.com <ggentile@ptd.net>
Sent: Friday, July 23, 2021 2:46:47 PM
To: Rustin Cassway <rcassway@demount.com>
Subject: Olinda (or not)

Rusty - I went through my Olinda folder today and found these numbers: 37-47.268 / 74-11.873. I think that you should plot these on a chart.

Gary Gentile 500 Lehigh Gorge Drive Jim Thorpe, PA 18229 252-394-6974 gary@ggentile.com Website: www.ggentile.com This message was sent with recycled electrons So many shipwrecks, so many mountains, so many rivers, so little time . . .

The only interest that was aroused occurred in August – eight months after I had identified the *U-111* – when Ben Roberts happened to casually mention my identification of the *U-111* to Erik Petkovic – and he has regretted it ever since. Petkovic called me immediately afterward and excitedly told me that he had never heard of the *U-111*, and that he knew nothing about it. He wanted me to copy my entire *U-111* folder and send it to him, along with all my photographs of the U-boat. He did not proffer compensation. I explained to him why I could not accept his generous offer; my *U-111* folder was still missing.

He also told me that he was going to visit me at home some time and copy all my World War 2 U-boat folders for a project of his.

The reason for Petkovic's lack of local shipwreck knowledge was due to his recent move from Ohio to the Washington, DC area. I don't know if he ever even dived on a wreck that lay off the eastern seaboard, or had technical diving skills. This is not to hold anything against him. It's just that he was new to Atlantic Ocean shipwreck diving, the same as I would be about Pacific Ocean diving if I moved to California.

I acknowledged that I was certain of the location and identity of the *U-111*. I told him how I had made the connection with the putative *R-8*, and that as far as I was concerned, everything that he needed to know had been published in my chapter in *Shipwrecks of Virginia* (1992), which included photographs of the *U-111* as well as the location that was given in the *Falcon's* deck log. Additional research was unnecessary. The only action needed now was to "go where the neoprene meets the water," as Ken Clayton used to say.

Somehow, Petkovic managed to inveigle himself onto the existing email chain that included Cassway, Roberts, and myself. Once he did that, he had access to the entire chain, and all the previous information that it contained.

Come autumn, Ben Roberts used another method of determining useful if negative information: the process of elimination. His primary purpose was, in his email words, "to research Gentile's theory that the sub wreck thought to be *R-8* (*Olinda*) was actually *U-111*." He accomplished this in two stages. First, in October, the National Archives "sent me station logs for the Philadelphia Navy Yard that identified USS *Cormorant* as the vessel that towed USS *R-8* out to be scuttled." Second, in December, the National Archives "sent me the *Cormorant's* deck logs, which revealed that the *R-8* was actually ~70 miles from the wreck it was thought to be (*Olinda*). The log also revealed that the *R-8* was sunk far beyond the edge of the continental shelf, placing it unambiguously in very deep water, well beyond the reach of all but the most sophisticated oceanographic equipment."

According to the *Cormorant's* log, "The U.S.S. *R-8* sank from the effects of bombing in 720 fathoms of water with Cape Henry Lighthouse bearing 282°-30', distance 71.5 miles." The number in fathoms equals 4,320 feet.

This meant that the *Olinda* wreck could not be the *R-8*, "and that the *Olinda* wreck must be another submarine."

This did not necessarily propose that the *Olinda* wreck had to *be* the *U-111*, but it certainly increased the odds that it was, especially as it was already known that the *U-111* had been scuttled very close to the site of the *Olinda* wreck, and that no other U-boats or submarines were known to have been lost in the vicinity. By process of elimination, archival confirmation of the *R-8's* location convinced Ben Roberts of the likelihood that the *Olinda* wreck was the *U-111*.

Thus, after twelve months of working to obtain acceptance of my identification proposal, the year closed with growing confidence from Roberts and Cassway that I had been correct all along.

Or, as Ben Roberts so firmly declared, "*This was the pivotal moment in which our effort to identify the site began . . . because it would 'literally re-write local dive history.'* "

Roberts: "At one point in the ensuing email discussion, Petkovic indicated that he believed the *U-111* rested in only 210' of water (which

N. Nav. 43
(Mar. 1929)

Page 421

UNITED STATES SHIP CORMORANT Tuesday 18 August, 1936
(Day.) (Date.) (Month.)

ZONE DESCRIPTION plus 5

REMARKS.

0 to 4.
Steaming on course 243°T 240 PGC 254°PSC at about 4 knots, 39 RPM with U.S.S. R-8 in tow astern. Senior officer present on U.S.S. OWL. Aver. steam 200 lbs. Ave. RPM 39.

E. DELAVY, Chief Boatswain, USN.

4 to 8.
Steaming as before on course 243°T, 240° PGC, 251° PSC. Standard speed 4 knots - 39 RPM. 0525 Shifted to a lighter tow line between Roger eight and ship. 0655 Changed course to 270° T, 267° PGC, 276° PSC. Aver. Steam 200 lbs. Aver. RPM 34.

H. PLANDER, Lieut., USN.

8 to 12.
Steaming on course 270°T, 267 PGC, 276 PSC, 3 knots 30 RPM. 0845 Aircraft task group arrived from Naval Air Station, Hampton Roads, Va. 0918 Commenced scheduled exercises in connection with bombing problem on U.S.S. R-8. 1st bomb dropped. 0952 Plane dropped second bomb. 1000 Plane dropped third bomb. 1030 Plane dropped fourth bomb. 1035 Observed R-8 settling by the bow. 1036 Plane dropped fifth bomb. 1108 Increased speed to 4.6 knots 35 RPM. 1110 Visibility much reduced planes ordered to base by SOP. 1120 Hauled down baker with U.S.S. OWL. Average steam 200. Average RPM 30.0

E. DELAVY, Chief Boatswain, USN.

12 to 16.
Steaming as before on course 270°T., 267°pgc., 276°psc., standard speed 3.6 knots(35RPM). 12:35 Changed speed to 4.1 knots(40RPM). 12:45 Changed course to 012°T., 009°pgc., 011°psc. 12:58 Changed course to 000°T., 357°pgc., 000°psc. 13:01 Changed speed to 3 knots(30RPM). 13:11 Changed speed to 4.1 knots(40RPM). 15:12 Changed speed to 3 knots(30RPM). 15:20 Shortened tow to 1000 feet. 15:52 Ahead 1/3 speed, standard speed 3 knots(30RPM). 15:59 Changed speed to 3.6 knots(35RPM). Average steam 200. Average RPM 37.2

R.S. HAZLETT, Chief Gunner, U.S. Navy.

16 to 20
Steaming as before. 16:19 changed course to 090°T., 087°pgc., 101°psc. 18:38 changed course to 060°T., 057°pgc., 068°psc. Average steam 200. Average RPM 34.

H. PLANDER, Lieutenant, U.S. Navy.

20 to 24
On course 060°T., 057°pgc., 068°psc, steaming at 3.6 knots to maintain station. U.S.S. R-8 in tow astern. Average steam 200 pounds. Average RPM 35.

E. DELAVY, Chief Boatswain, U.S. Navy.

Approved: Examined:
H. PLANDER
Lieutenant, U.S. Navy.
Commanding & Navigator.
U. S. N., Navigator.

(Original (ribbon) copy of this page to be sent to Bureau of Navigation monthly.)

N. Nav. 48
(Mar. 1920)

Page 473

UNITED STATES SHIP CORMORANT Wednesday 19 August 1936
(Day.) (Date.) (Month.)

ZONE DESCRIPTION plus 5.

REMARKS.

0 to 4.
Steaming on course 060°T, 057°PGC, 068°PSC. Standard speed 3.6 knots (35 RPM) with U.S.S. R-8 in tow astern with 2500 feet of 1" cable, in company with U.S.S. OWL (SOPA). 0200 Changed course to 180°T, 177°PGC, 195°PSC. Average steam 200 lbs. Average RPM 31.6

R.S. Hazlett
R.S. HAZLETT, Chief Gunner, USN.

4 to 8.
Steaming as before on course 180°T, 177°PGC, 195°PSC speed 4.1 knots (40 RPM). Average steam 200 pounds. Average RPM 36.

H. Plander
H. PLANDER, Lieut., USN.

8 to 12.
Steaming on base course 180°T, 177°PGC, 195°PSC., changing heading as needed to maintain uncontrolable tow astern during bombing operation. Speed 3.6 knots (35RPM). 0826 Commenced scheduled exercises. Plane dropped first bomb. 0834 Plane dropped second bomb. 0856 Plane dropped third bomb. 0920 Plane dropped fourth bomb. 0940 Plane dropped fifth bomb, bomb did not explode. 0949 Plane dropped sixth bomb. 1004 Plane dropped seventh bomb. 1025 Aircraft task group returned to base. 1100 Target observed to be sinking slowly. 1125 The U.S.S. R-8 sank from the effects of bombing in 720 fathoms of water with Cape Henry Lighthouse bearing 282°-30', distance 71.5 miles. 1140 Transferred rake party personnel to U.S.S. OWL; Lieutenant (jg) W.M. Walsh, U.S. Navy; M.P. Bradford, Plc, U.S.Navy; T.L. Wilfong AMM3c, U.S.Navy. 1140 Exercises in connection with the R-8 completed. 1146 Proceeding to Naval Mine Depot, Yorktown, Virginia, course 285°T, 282°PGC, 291°PSC., standard speed 12 knots (128RPM). 1155 Ahead full speed. 1204 Changed speed to 11.1 knots (110RPM)

R.S. Hazlett
R.S. HAZLETT, Chief Gunner, USN.

12 to 16.
Steaming on course 285°T, 282°PGC, 291PSC, speed 11 knots (110RPM). Before parting company with U.S.S. OWL, Philip Patrick Cloonan, CBM(pa) was placed aboard that vessel for transportation to Hampton Roads and transfer to Receiving Station, N.O.B., for further transfer to Fleet Reserve. 1240 Changed speed to 12.7 knots (128RPM). 1400 Changed course to 275°T, 277°PGC, 290°PSC. 1418 Changed course to 285°T, 282°PGC, 271°PSC. Average steam 200 pounds. Average RPM 124.1

H. Plander
H. PLANDER, Lieut., USN.

16 to 20.
Steaming as before. 1612 Changed course to 288°T, 285°PGC, 294°PSC. 1649 Passed Chesapeake light vessel abeam to starboard; distance 450 yards. 1725 Changed course to 265°T, 263°PGC, 273°PSC. 1756 Changed course to 283°T, 280°PGC, 288°PSC. 1802 Changed course to 293°T, 290°PGC, 298°PSC. 1805 Changed course to 313°T, 310°PGC, 316°PSC. 1807 Gas buoy #6 abeam to starboard; distance 200 yards. At 1905 with York River Entrance fairway can buoy abeam to port close aboard, commenced steering various courses to conform to the York River Channel. 1922 Passed York Spit Light abeam to starboard, distance .7 miles. 1950 Tue Marshes Light abeam to port, distance 800 yards. Average steam 200. Average RPM 128.

H. Plander
H. PLANDER, Lieut., USN.

Approved: H. Plander
H. PLANDER,
Lieutenant, U.S.Navy,
Commanding and Navigator.

Examined:
U. S. N., Navigator.

(Original (ribbon) copy of this page to be sent to Bureau of Navigation monthly.)

would place it at least 10 miles from the true wreck site) . . . In other words, he had no prior knowledge of *U-111's* actual location.

"On December 21, 2021, I told Gentile that I had 60% confidence that *U-111* had been found but misidentified."

On December 30, 2021, Roberts wrote, "The appropriate next step

The conning tower of the *U-111*. (Courtesy of the National Archives.)

is to obtain some underwater footage of the site (perhaps a ROV dive in the spring to start with?)"

A year had passed since I had identified the *U-111*. I was no closer to physical confirmation than I was twelve months earlier. But with Roberts' imprimatur, my long-lost U-boat was getting closer to the front burner: so close that Cassway finally took an interest in exploring it.

Once again, Ben Roberts came to the rescue.

Ben Roberts obtained this picture of the *Falcon's* deck log from the National Archives. This is the same log book from which I acquired the lat/lon of the *U-111's* scuttling site for use in *Shipwrecks of Virginia* (1992).

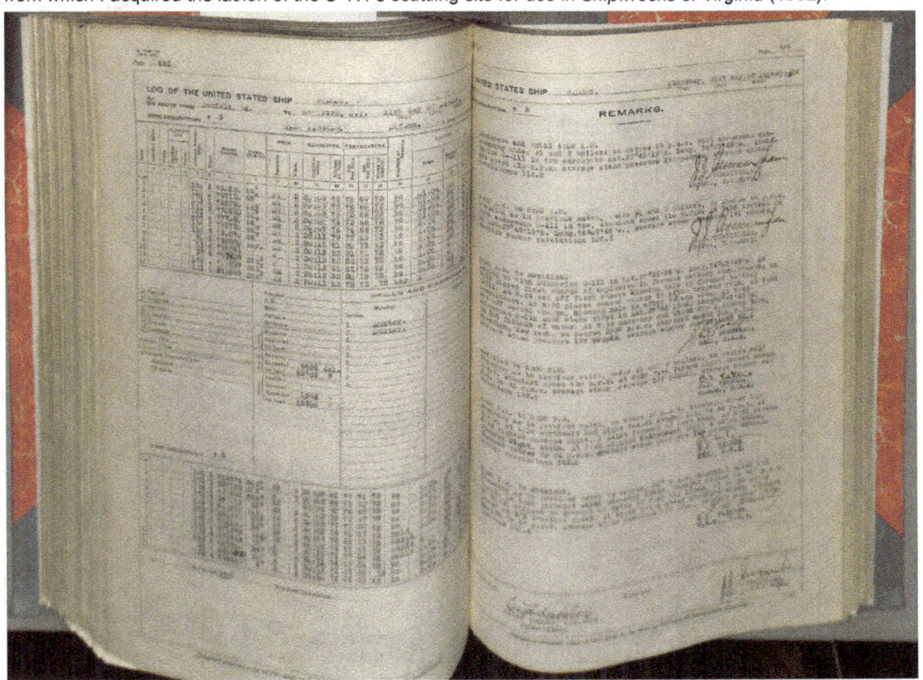

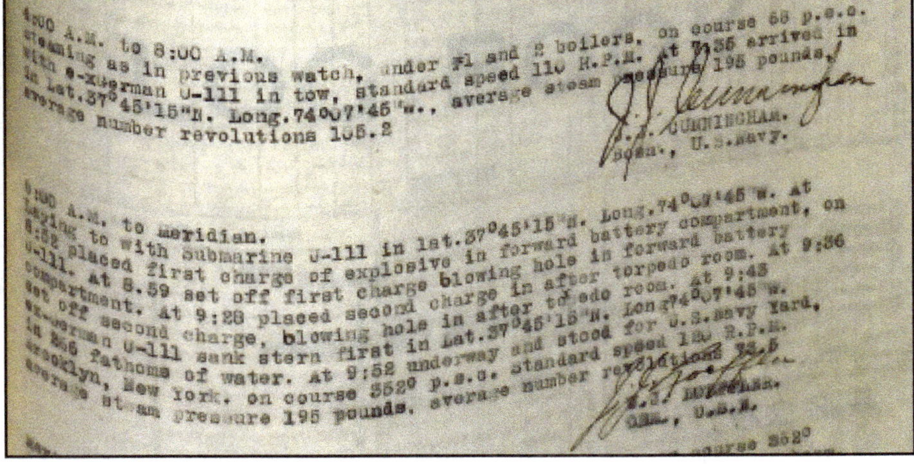

4:00 A.M. to 8:00 A.M.
Steaming as in previous watch, under #1 and 2 boilers, on course 68 p.s.c.
with ex-German U-111 in tow, standard speed 110 R.P.M. At 7:35 arrived in
in Lat.37°45'15"N. Long.74°07'45"W., average steam pressure 195 pounds,
average number revolutions 105.2

J.J. CUNNINGHAM.
Bosn., U.S.Navy.

8:00 A.M. to meridian.
Laying to with Submarine U-111 in lat.37°45'15"N. Long.74°07'45"W. at
8:52 placed first charge of explosive in forward battery compartment, on
U-111. At 8.59 set off first charge blowing hole in forward battery
compartment. At 9:28 placed second charge in after torpedo room. At 9:36
set off second charge, blowing hole in after torpedo room. At 9:48
ex-German U-111 sank stern first in Lat.37°45'15"N. Long.74°07'45"W.
in 856 fathoms of water. At 9:52 underway and stood for U.S.Navy Yard,
Brooklyn, New York. on course 352° p.s.c. standard speed 120 R.P.M.
average steam pressure 195 pounds. average number revolutions 93.5

E.J. [illegible]
CBM., U.S.N.

course 352°

In the foreground, the U.S. submarine *S-2* is making a trial submergence. The conning tower of the U-111 appears in the background. This photograph was taken at the Portsmouth Navy Yard, in Portsmoiuth, New Hampshire.

(Courtesy of the National Archives.)

In the spring of 2022, Ben Roberts contacted Ross Baxter and informed him that I had identified the *U-111*. Baxter owned and operated a remotely operated vehicle that could reach the depth of the wreck. The ROV was equipped with a video camera and flood lights. Roberts wanted Baxter to obtain the visual proof that was needed to confirm the wreck's identity. Baxter agreed to provide his ROV, expertise, and personal service flying the vehicle, all without charge.

With the ROV on board, Roberts proceeded to organize a trip.

By now there was so much evidence that the *Olinda* wreck could not possibly be the *R-8*, and that it almost certainly had to be the *U-111*, that Rusty Cassway's previous indifference yielded to the strength of the circumstantial evidence, perhaps with the notion of having the identity of the submarine - the eastern seaboard's only World War 1 U-boat that was yet unaccounted for - established by the use of his boat. The bragging rights alone were worth their weight in platinum. His change in attitude was essential because his was the only dive charter vessel that was available for such an offshore journey.

Or was it? (Again?)

The bad news was that Cassway sold his boat. The good news was that he was having another, and larger, boat built . . . but that construction delays were keeping it out of the water. Instead of being ready by spring, the new boat was not completed and taken for a shake-down cruise until the beginning of summer.

Subject	U-111
From	Rustin Cassway <rcassway@demount.com>
To	gary <gary@ggentile.com>, Ben Roberts <johnbenroberts@gmail.com>
Date	Sunday June 12, 2022 9:48:33 AM

Gary

I would like to invite you on the maiden adventure of the new boat to survey the U-111 by way of Remote Operated Vehicle

This will happen in the next week or so

Give me a call

As you can read, there was no doubt in Cassway's mind that we were going to see for ourselves the wreck of the *U-111*. I viewed this new attitude as a sincere vote of confidence in my identification of the wreck: an identification that was now a year and a half old.

I called, and told him that my schedule was clear so that I could make the trip no matter which departure date he chose. He kept me constantly updated. In the mean time, he organized a team to accompany us on the historic trip. There would be no diving.

Now that I was certain that the *U-111* confirmation trip was in the works, I began the process of organizing my notes and creating an outline about how I could best tell the story in the form of a book. My background material went back to the early 1980's, when I first learned

The *Miss Lindsey* was owned and operated by Mike Hillier, who also owned the Lynnhaven Diver Center in Virginia Beach, Virginia. The *Miss Lindsey* was our sole means of transportation to the Billy Mitchell Wrecks for the entire length of the project. No other operators had the courage to take us to wrecks which the certifying agencies claimed was too deep and dangerous to dive. The boat was named after Hillier's daughter Lindsey, who as a pre-teen sometimes crewed for us and stood nighttime watches. She now owns and operates the dive shop after Hillier's passing.

about the German warships that were appropriated by the U.S. Navy. At that time, I had made hand-written notes which I quickly set aside when I learned the depth at which the vessels had been scuttled.

To recapitulate, in 1989, I brought those notes out of mothballs when I started work in earnest on my Popular Dive Guide Series. That was the year when I commenced intensive research about Billy Mitchell (at the Library of Congress) and what I started calling the Billy Mitchell Wrecks (at the National Archives and the Naval Historical Center).

In 1990, Ken Clayton and I launched our seven-year project to locate and dive on the German wrecks. The only one that we did not find was the *U-111*, due to its accidental sinking, prolonged salvage, and eventual scuttling in what the records misinformed us was extremely deep water off the Continental Shelf. In those days, Ken and I were making dives to depths in the range of (and deeper than) 390 feet. Our deepest dive was 420 feet, on the cruiser *Frankfurt*. Had we not been misled by the wrongly recorded depth and location, we would have searched for the *U-111* and dived on it in the 1990's.

Now, more than four decades later, I was prepared to tell her story in context with the three U-boats that we had located and explored. This would complete a project that Ken and I had started but did not complete until 2022. Better late than never, as the saying goes.

My only wish was that Ken Clayton were still alive to witness the momentous conclusion to our Billy Mitchell Wreck project. He and I had been out of touch for a number of years, each having gone our own way through lives that were dictated by personal objectives. Clayton was a brilliant computer analyst who held government jobs that required a security clearance for Top Secret Compartmented Information. Whenever I asked him what kind of work he did, he responded not-so-jokingly, "I can tell you, but then I would have to kill you." Under those circumstances, I decided that I did not need to know what kind of work he did for Uncle Sam.

According to his obituary, he passed away from Alzheimer's disease in 2017. He was 79 years old. An African proverb was displayed at his memorial service: "When an old man dies, a library burns to the ground." That was certainly true for him, for during his prime he had a mind that placed him in the top one percentile of human intellect.

More important than his intelligence quotient was his drive in whatever he did, for the government or in his hobbies. He was a master chess player and an expert whitewater rafter before he started deep-water wreck-diving.

We had worked together so hard to bring the Billy Mitchell Wrecks into the limelight that I almost felt that he was with me at the present time – at least in my heart – when I ultimately deciphered the *U-111's* identity, and learned that the wreck lay at a depth at which we could have dived on it when we were diving on the other German warships.

If only we had known. . . .

One sour note in our efforts to find all the Billy Mitchell Wrecks was that years afterward, NOAA (National Oceanic and Atmospheric Association) purchased *Shipwrecks of Virginia*, used my published coordinates to locate first the *Ostfriesland* and afterward the other Billy Mitchell Wrecks, then published a press release in which NOAA claimed to have "discovered" them. Neither Ken Clayton nor I were mentioned as predecessors and first divers on the wrecks. Was NOAA so desperate for acclaim that it had to steal it from the true finders?

Another sour note applied only to me. Due to increasing pain and worsening disabilities from my combat wounds, I was no longer able to dive to the depths of the *U-111*. Or to any depth, for that matter. My diving career ended on July 10, 2011, after my 200th dive on the *Andrea Doria* . . . when I had to be hauled onto the boat in screaming pain like a half-dead beached whale. It signaled the end of my diving career.

The date for the ROV dive was finally set for June 22, 2022. Unfortunately, Ben Roberts could not make the trip due to a scheduling conflict. To make it more convenient for me, Cassway arranged for me to meet Ross Baxter at his home in Warrington, Pennsylvania (an hour away from my home), then to carpool with him to Cape May, New Jersey. Also carpooling with us were Jon Haws (who had dived on the *Olinda* the previous year) and his grown son Michael (not yet a diver).

These three men were strangers to me, yet they knew all about me. They had read my books, knew about my diving career in general, and in particular about my mixed-gas dives on the Billy Mitchell Wrecks, including the three U-boats that Ken Clayton and I had found and dived. They had plenty of questions to ask not only about the *U-111* but about other east-coast shipwrecks. We did not lack for conversation during the two-and-a-half-hour drive to Cape May, New Jersey.

They wanted to hear all about the *U-111*, of course, but they were also interested in other U-boats and American submarines that were under my weight belt. I was somewhat of a submarine expert as I had dived on and written magazine articles and book chapters about so many of them. I knew about all of them.

Long ago I found that I could not learn anything by talking, because I already knew everything that I had to say. I wanted to listen to my fellow divers. So we had a conversational tug-of-war: they kept asking me questions and I kept trying to sneak in queries of my own.

One item of special interest to me was a fact that Baxter happened to mention: that he had positively identified a tanker about which I had speculated in my books. The *Oklahoma* broke in two in 1914; the two sections separated and drifted apart, finally sinking several days later some one hundred miles away from each other. Both sections were

Towing machinery on the stern of the *Oklahoma*, showing the cable wound onto its drum. Atop the overhead to the left is a life ring stamped with the vessel's name and first port of registry: Port Arthur, Texas. To the right are dual docking telegraphs, the auxiliary helm, and a compass binnacle. (From the author's collection.)

being dived but their true nature as sections of the *Oklahoma* was largely unknown.

Baxter had dived on the stern section and videotaped the towing machinery and cable drum, which look exactly as they looked in contemporary photographs of the stern, which I published in *Shipwrecks of New Jersey: South* and *Shipwrecks of Delaware and Maryland.* I congratulated him on his positive identification.

Haws was reticent but I was finally able to get him to talk a little about his dive on the *Olinda.* He was casual about a dive which had a four-hour run-time, while I was in awe about a dive to 330 feet with half an hour bottom time.

Baxter and Haws were prime examples of the new generation of technical divers: those who were diving deeper and staying longer than the technical divers of yesteryear. Both employed rebreathers to furnish the proper mix of oxygen, nitrogen, and helium. All my mixed-gas dives, including the dive to 420 feet on the German cruiser *Frankfurt,* I made with old-fashioned cylinders, which are now passe for long deep dives.

We arrived at Cassway's shore house where we were assigned sleeping quarters. This was where I met that night's bunkmate, Dan Quinlan. He had been a captain in the National Guard, while I had been a lowly private in the Army, so that then and during the next day on the ocean, I made mock salutes to him, and he returned them with mockery. I did not call him sir.

We were rudely awakened at oh dark hundred. The marina where Cassway kept his boat was fifteen minutes away. On dive trips, loading the boat is a long and arduous process because divers had so much dive gear to carry onboard. This trip was different. The only big items were Baxter's ROV and cable reel. Soon we were headed out to sea for a 75-mile boat ride.

On the boat I was introduced to another crewmember, Jim Walsh. He was a twenty-year Army veteran who had been a Huey pilot in Vietnam. Yet despite our related military backgrounds, we did not discuss our combat experiences, but instead stayed focused on the issue at hand: the *U-111.*

I brought a book to read for the ride out and back, but spent nearly every minute exchanging information with the crewmembers. The excitement on the boat was palpable. There was no doubt in anyone's mind that we were going to see a U-boat through the lens of Baxter's video camera, which was mounted on the ROV.

I had waited for this day for a year and a half. I had no qualms. I was positive that we were going to see the *U-111* in four to five hours. Therefore my attitude was casual.

What surprised me was that everyone else onboard was just as positive that we were going to the *U-111.* I did not know some of these people. They knew me only by reputation. Yet they were willing to take my word that the *U-111* was located precisely where I said it was going to be. They were so positive about this historic event in which they were involved, that they were each willing to contribute $375 for the cost of fuel. That displayed a great deal of confidence in my promise to show them the last unidentified World War One 1 U-boat on the entire eastern seaboard.

Another crewmember was a long-time dive buddy with whom I had shared many experiences; most diving but also mountain biking. His name was John Copeland. He was a retired truck mechanic.

Last but least was Erik Petkovic: a close friend of Rusty Cassway. Too close, as it happened.

I was not asked to pay because I was an honored guest who had given Cassway this unique opportunity on a silver platter. I could have given it to Mazraani, who had first side-scanned the wreck site: an action that had enabled me - because of my previous research - to make the correct identification.

I chose to give the opportunity to Cassway because I thought that he was my friend.

There was so much ongoing conversation that the four-hour boat ride passed with celerity. Suddenly the engine revolutions were reduced. Then the boat pirouetted as Cassway piloted the boat in a pattern that enabled him to locate the target with the depth recorder. Ted Green's "numbers" were right on the spot. It took but a few minutes to draw a pattern of the wreck, and position the boat over top of the conning tower.

Jon Haws pulled anchor line out of the rope locker in preparation for dropping the grapnel onto the hull.

Cassway tooted the horn. Haws tossed the grapnel overboard and paid out line as the grapnel sank to the bottom. He kept paying out line for quite a while. Not just 390 feet of line to reach the bottom, but enough line so that the boat could drift back in order to allow the flukes

Waiting for the "hook' to grab (from left to right): Jon Haws, John Copeland, Jim Walsh.

In the wheelhouse, Ross Baxter is seated (left), prepared to issue orders to the deck crew on the bow; notice the microphone in his hand. Michael Haws is standing behind him (face on the right).

to grab onto the hull and create a comfortable catenary with the scope. Minutes passed. In the wheelhouse, the skipper watched the target move off the screen. He tooted for Haws to pull in the grapnel.

This was not an unusual situation. A grapnel often did not snag a chunk of wreckage on its initial pass – or on several more passes. On some shipwrecks a smooth hull did not present projections that could catch a grapnel's fluke. On other wrecks a grapnel grabbed wreckage that was not strong enough to

Dan Quinlan is not simply overseeing ROV deployment operations. He is watching for approaching vessels. While we were anchored, one fishing vessel passed close aport, and a large tanker in the distance crossed the bow. (In this case, "bow" refers to the front of the boat; it is also half of a dog's bark.)

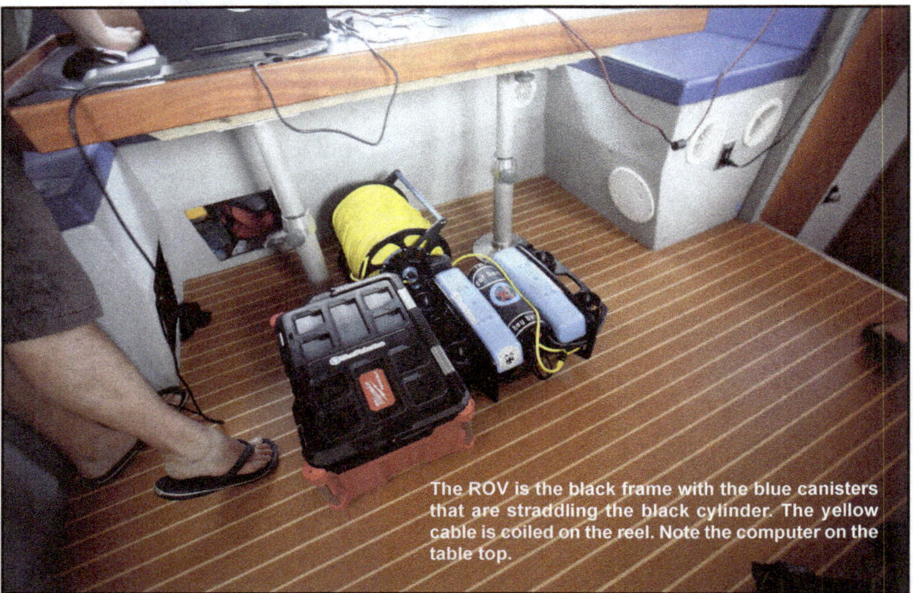
The ROV is the black frame with the blue canisters that are straddling the black cylinder. The yellow cable is coiled on the reel. Note the computer on the table top.

hold the boat without breaking free. Submarines were particularly difficult to "hook" because the hull was curved and rounded, in which case a grapnel could slide completely over the hull without finding a rough place to catch. The situation could be catch as catch can, if you will pardon a pun on a cliché.

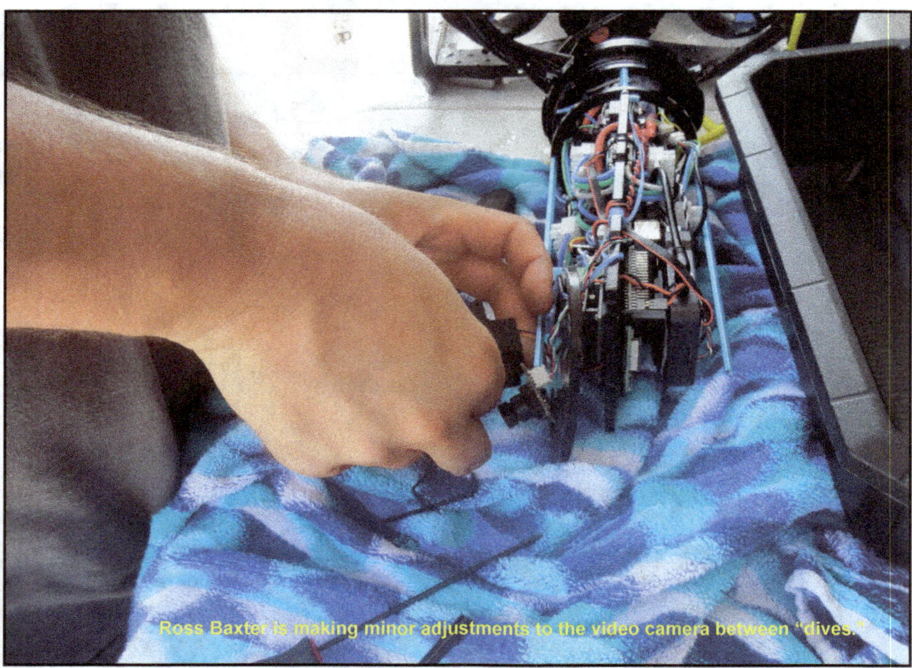
Ross Baxter is making minor adjustments to the video camera between "dives."

Jon Haws deploys the ROV as John Copeland feeds the cable from the reel. It was necessary to keep the cable taut so it not get wrapped around the boat's propeller.

The second drop was more successful. The line grew taut, did not pull free, then became as tight as a violin string so that it sang in the current. The grapnel held.

Now it was Baxter's turn to get to work. He had already prepared the ROV, attached the cable, connected the onboard electronics, and tested the devices to ensure that everything was functioning. He sat in the cabin (which contained the galley, a U-shaped sofa, a long table, a

The image in the remote monitor in the upper right corner is the image that Ross Baxter is seeing on the computer screen.

Ross Baxter "flying" the ROV from inside the cabin.

Towing the ROV to the bow.

ladder up to the wheelhouse, and steps down the head (rest room to landlubbers) and a sleeping compartment.

My station was next to him so that I could see the computer screen where the underwater images would be displayed. My job was to compare my photographs of the *U-111* with the structural components on the deck of the hull.

Crewmembers hoisted the ROV over the starboard rail, then lowered it into the water and unreeled the cable as it was needed. Baxter controlled the unit by means of a video game controller which he adapted for convenience. The way he steered the ROV was by visual input from the video camera. He was looking for the hull of the boat but saw nothing but empty ocean. He kept turning the unit in circles in the hope of catching a glimpse of the hull so he would know the direction in which to steer. He saw nothing but empty ocean no matter which way he turned.

I stood up and looked out the window. I could not see the ROV but I saw the yellow cable stretched perpendicular to the boat. "Ross, the ROV is a hundred yards off the starboard side."

To make the dive, Baxter had to get the boat's hull in view, then follow it to the bow so he could follow the anchor line down to the wreck.

By this time, after fighting the strong surface current for ten minutes or more, the charge on the battery was too low to make the dive. Exasperated, he shouted for the crew to reel in the unit. This was soon accomplished. Baxter removed the battery and plugged it into the charger. He then installed the backup battery so he could start the next dive with a battery that was fully charged.

The crewmembers put their collective heads together and developed a method to get the ROV to the bow without using battery power. They carried it. Then they used a boat hook to lower the unit into the water. After the ROV was submerged, Baxter drove it forward until he could see the anchor line. The surface current was still strong, so he closed the unit's articulated claw around the anchor line. This way he could not lose sight of the line. Plus, he used just enough battery power to offset the current, and let gravity pull the unit down the line. Once the ROV got deeper than the surface current, forward movement was easier to maintain. There was still the friction of moving water against the cable, but the cable presented less surface area than the body of the ROV.

The computer screen displayed the depth of the ROV. Baxter kept calling out the numbers as the unit settled deeper into the water. The ROV slid down the line as if it were a roller coaster on a track. Abruptly, it bumped against the bottom at 390 feet, and stirred a thin cloud of sand and silt. Baxter released the claw and backed away from the anchor line, then started ascending alongside the encrusted hull.

The ROV rose slowly until it reached the top of the hull. The image was not crystal clear due to particulate matter in the water. The matter reflected light from the video camera's bulbs. This made each piece of matter look like a tiny light emitting diode, or LED. Current pushed the matter past the lens, but did not obstruct the grander image of the shipwreck beyond the dots of light. Twisted strands of a fishing net loomed above the opposite side of the hull.

Courtesy of the Naval Photographic Center.

Baxter propelled the ROV slowly along the upper edge of the hull. A shadowy shape appeared in the near distance. As the camera moved closer to the shape, it quickly resolved itself into the conning tower of a submarine. It was a perfect match for the conning tower on the photograph in my book that I was holding in my hand.

Quietly I said, "It's the *U-111*."

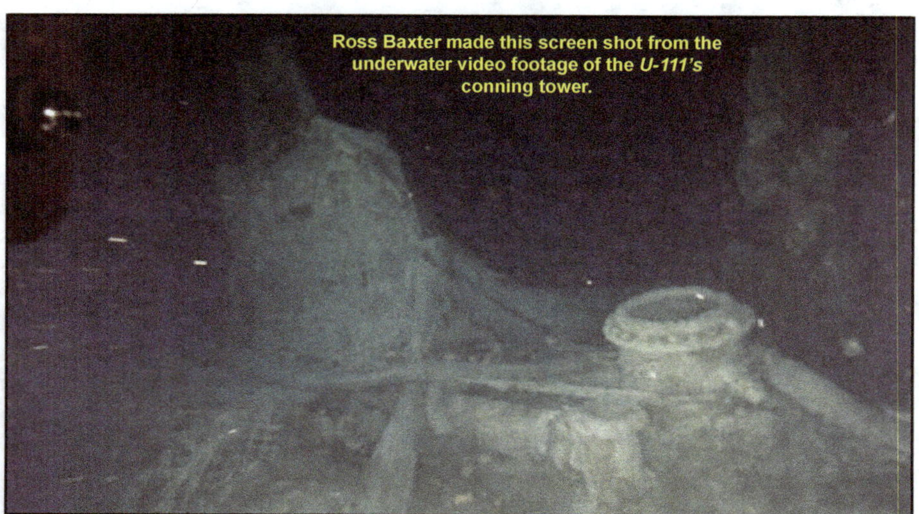

Ross Baxter made this screen shot from the underwater video footage of the *U-111's* conning tower.

Back at the dock after a successful trip to the long lost *U-111*.
Left: The author and identifier.
Right: Ross Baxter and corroborater.

A cheer arose in the cabin with the realization that our mission had been accomplished. The faith that the crew had held for me had just been proven. I breathed deeply.

But the dive was not over. Baxter continued to propel the ROV along the hull until it reached another recognizable feature: a gun platform that was also shown on the photograph. By rotating the ROV, Baxter moved it in the opposite direction until it passed the conning tower and reached the other gun platform that was shown on the photograph.

In the process of making this maneuver, the ROV's cable got tangled around something that was out of sight. There were some anxious moments as Baxter moved the $12,000 unit back and forth and up and down in an attempt to free it from entanglement. Baxter remained calm – at least, he looked calm to me – and kept maneuvering the ROV until the loop in its cable slipped off a projection and he zoomed away from

The *U-111* was a Type *U-93* U-boat. Ben Roberts compared the Type *U-93* construction plans (below left) with his side-scan sonar image (below right). This enables viewers who are unfamiliar with U-boat designs and layouts to match features on the plans with equivalent features on the sunken submarine. On the following page (right) he indicated some of the more prominent features of the wreck by having arrows point to the location of those features.

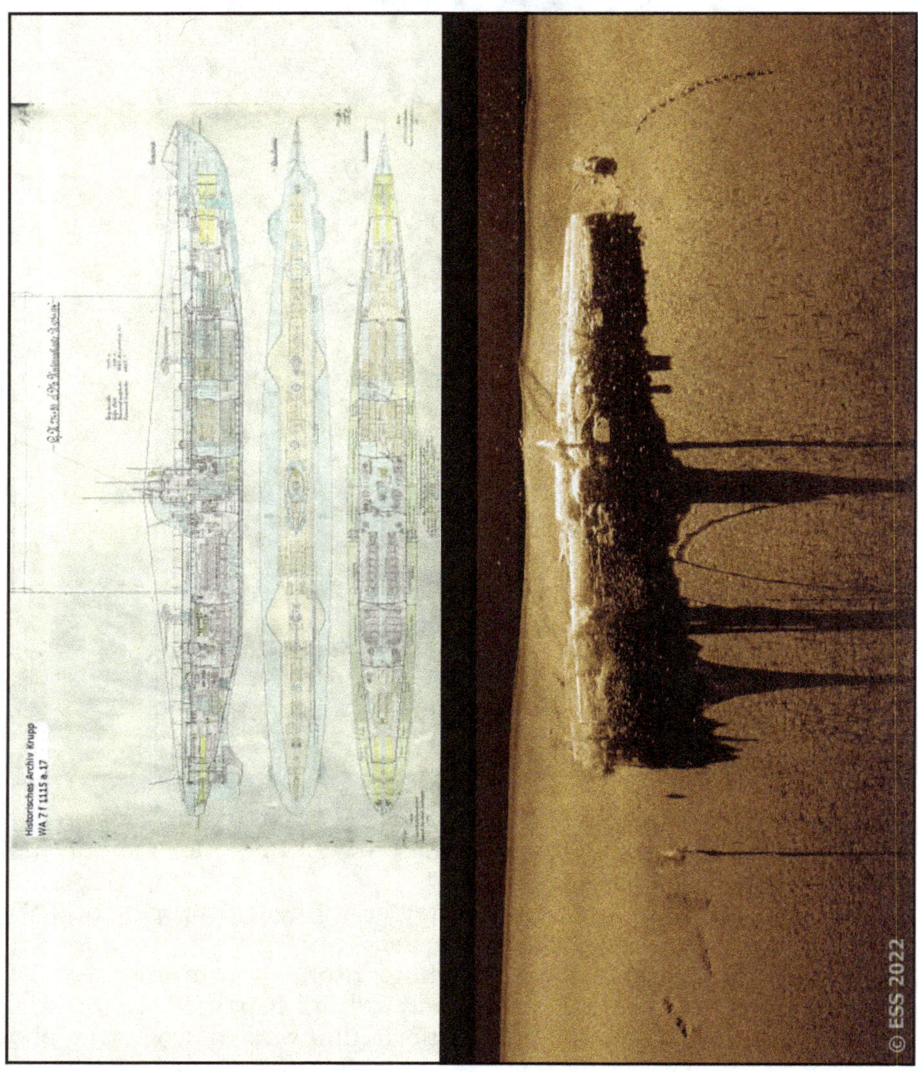

Ben Roberts obtained the construction plans from Friedrich Krupp Germaniawerft, in Germany. During World War 1, Krupp built 84 U-boats for the German navy. The Krupp family business has been in existence for more than four centuries. If you are interested in knowing more about Krupp, as the company is commonly called, read *Merchants of Death* by H. C. Ehgelgrecht and F. C. Hanighen. The company has had a long history in developing steel, armor, armament, and artillery. Today it makes kitchen accessories such as dishwashers and coffee makers.

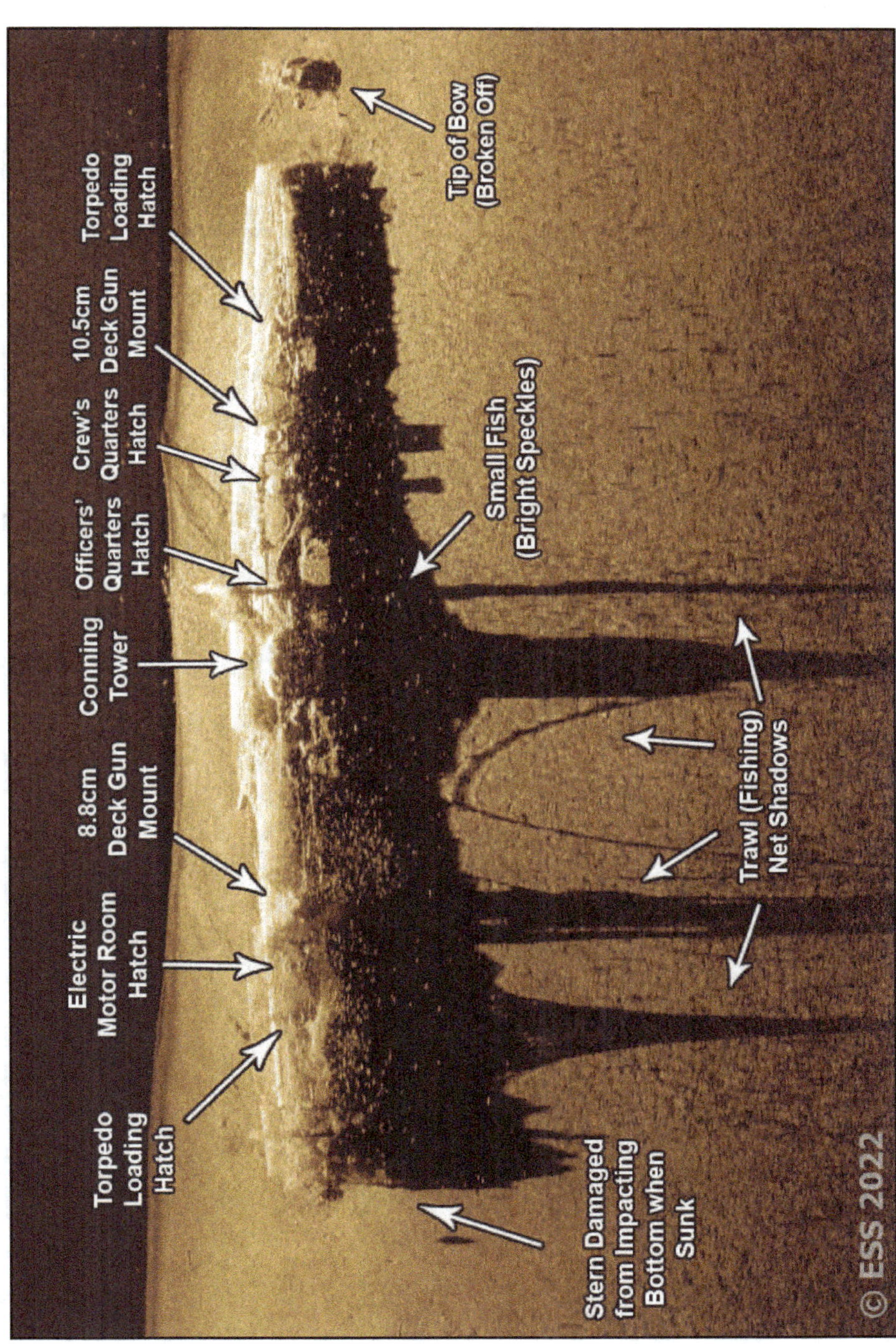
Tip of Bow (Broken Off)
Torpedo Loading Hatch
10.5cm Deck Gun Mount
Crew's Quarters Hatch
Officers' Quarters Hatch
Conning Tower
8.8cm Deck Gun Mount
Electric Motor Room Hatch
Torpedo Loading Hatch
Small Fish (Bright Speckles)
Trawl (Fishing) Net Shadows
Stern Damaged from Impacting Bottom when Sunk
© ESS 2022

U-111 along side a pier. The flag beneath the American Stars and Stripes is a contemporary German flag. (Courtesy of the National Archives.)

the U-boat . . . else the ROV might have been another U-boat victim.

Baxter had enough footage to identify the *U-111*, so he terminated the dive and headed the unit for the surface. Crewmembers reeled in the cable as the ROV ascended. Soon the unit was on the surface, from which point the crew hauled in the cable as they coiled it around the drum of the reel. They lifted the ROV out of the water and placed it safely on the deck.

Baxter was the hero of the day!

After the grapnel was pulled free of the wreckage, we headed for the dock at high speed – a four-hour drive in fairly calm seas. As they say in the movie business: It's a wrap.

Back at the dock, I spotted Cassway and Petkovic whispering in a corner of the cabin. Cassway's back was toward me. As I approached them I heard the word "newspaper." Petkovic looked up at me. Cassway spun around and told me that Petkovic had a friend who had connections and might be able to get the story of the *U-111* published. I nodded, and said that I thought it was a good idea to seek publicity.

Cassway let Petkovic take responsibility for a press release.

Ben Roberts was not completely satisfied with the video footage identification. He wrote to the Krupp archives in Germany, from which he obtained a copy of the construction plans of the *U-111's* type (*U-93*).

He then took his boat to the wreck site - the *Olinda* wreck that had been misidentified as the American submarine *R-8* - and did a side-scan sonar survey from various angles. His imagery depicted in great detail the entire hull and the superstructure of the U-boat, as well as the fishing nets that adorned the hull. If anyone doubted that the wreck was that of the *U-111*, that doubt was permanently erased by his close-up side-scan sonar images, complete with descriptions of the various features and the way those features matched those that were shown on the construction plans.

The wreck was definitely not the *R-8*. In addition to the matching contours of the U-boat's conning tower and all other external features, the hull measured 49 feet longer than the hull of the American submarine. The length of the *R-8* was 186 feet, while the length of the *U-111* was 235 feet.

Ben Roberts was the hero of another day!

Here is a recapitulation of seminal events about the discovery and identification of the *U-111*:

1979: Wreck was "hung by trawl fisherman" and reported on AWOIS.
2018: Ted Green acquired GPS co-ordinates from commercial angler.
2020 December: Joe Mazraani side-scanned wreck, claimed as *R-8*.
2021 January: Spurred by Mazraani's side-scan sonar images, Gary Gentile concluded that the wreck was the *U-111*.
2022 June 22: Ross Baxter's video footage confirmed the *U-111*.
2022 September: Ben Roberts made high-resolution side-scan sonar images of the wreck site, further confirming Gentile's identification.

Months later, both paper and Internet news media went viral by offering stories of the discovery of the *U-111* to hundreds of thousands, perhaps millions, of gullible readers, not only in the United States and its territories but all over the world.

Every account was slightly different, was written by a different staff member, was printed in different words, was translated into different languages (including French, Spanish, Italian, German, Indonesian, Czechoslovakian, and others), but the story was always the same.

Here is an example from India:

thehansindia.com/offbeat/old-german-u-boat-wreck-from-world-war-i-was-discovered-by

THE HANS INDIA LATEST NEWS HYDERABAD NEWS ENTERTAINMENT CRICKET PHOTO STOR

One hundred years after being sunk in US waters, a German U-Boat submarine from World War I has been located. Eric Petkovic, a historian, shipwreck researcher, and expert wreck diver, found the shipwreck, known as U-boat U-111 marine.

The US Navy sank the U-111, the final German U-Boat submarine from World War I, off the coast of Virginia in 1922. The submarine sank at a depth of 1,600 feet. Petkovic unexpectedly found it in about 400 feet of water. Surprisingly, it was found in barely 400 feet of water off the coast of Virginia, much shallower than anticipated but still outside the range of human diving for all but a few highly skilled technical divers.

THE END

Or is it?

U-111 (From the author's collection)

U-111 (From the author's collection)

U-111 (From the author's collection)

B.C.O. 1056

U-111 (From the author's collection)

E.B.CO.1061

E.B.CO.1062

U-111 (From the author's collection)

U-111 (From the author's collection)

U-111 (From the author's collection)

U-111 (From the author's collection)

B.CO. 1067

U-111 (From the author's collection)

E.B.CO.1071

U-111 (From the author's collection)

U-111 (From the author's collection)

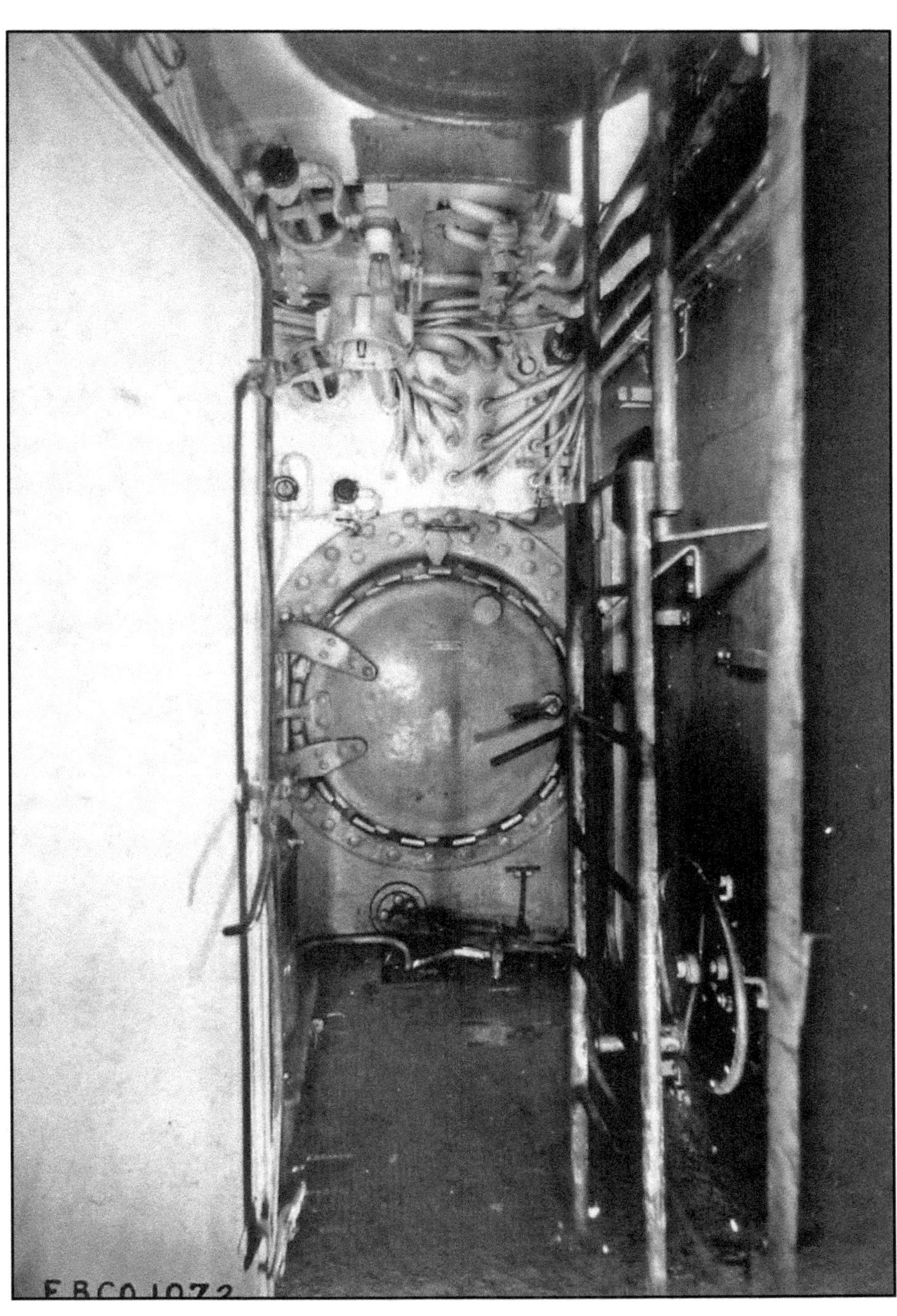

U-111 (From the author's collection)

E.B.CO.1074

U-111 (From the author's collection)

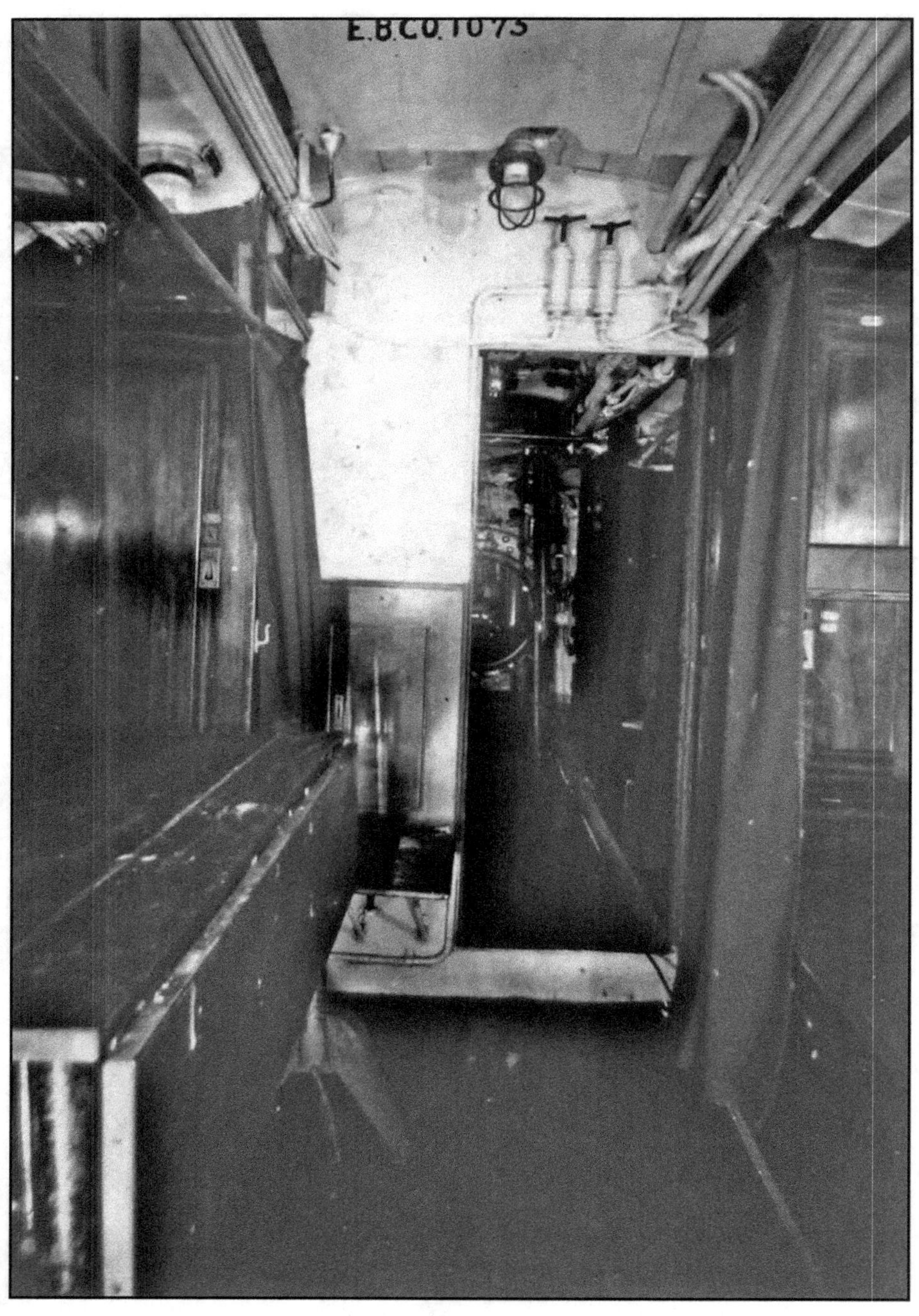

U-111 (From the author's collection)

E.B.CO. 1078

U-111 (From the author's collection)

U-111 (From the author's collection)

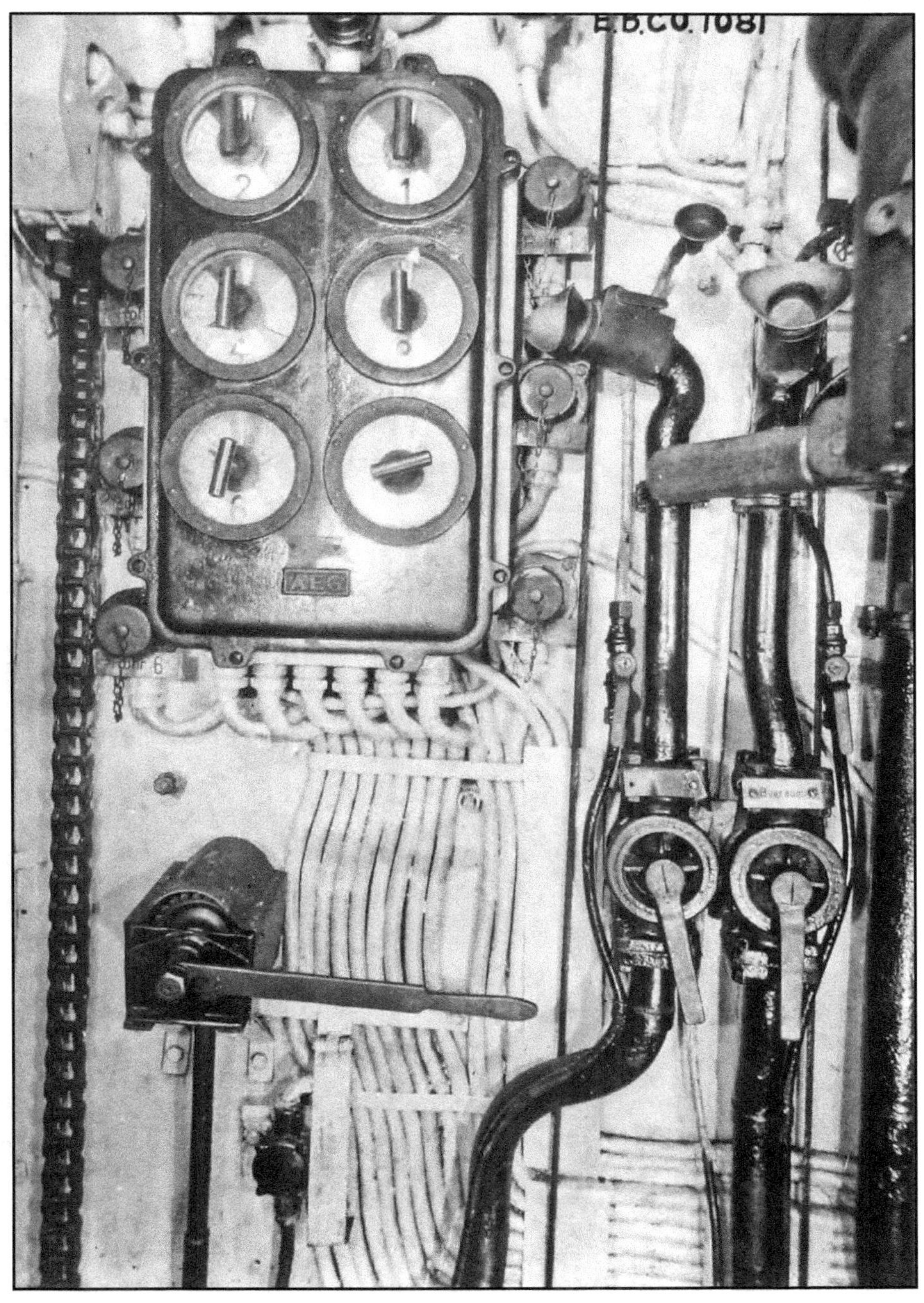

U-111 (From the author's collection)

U-111 (From the author's collection)

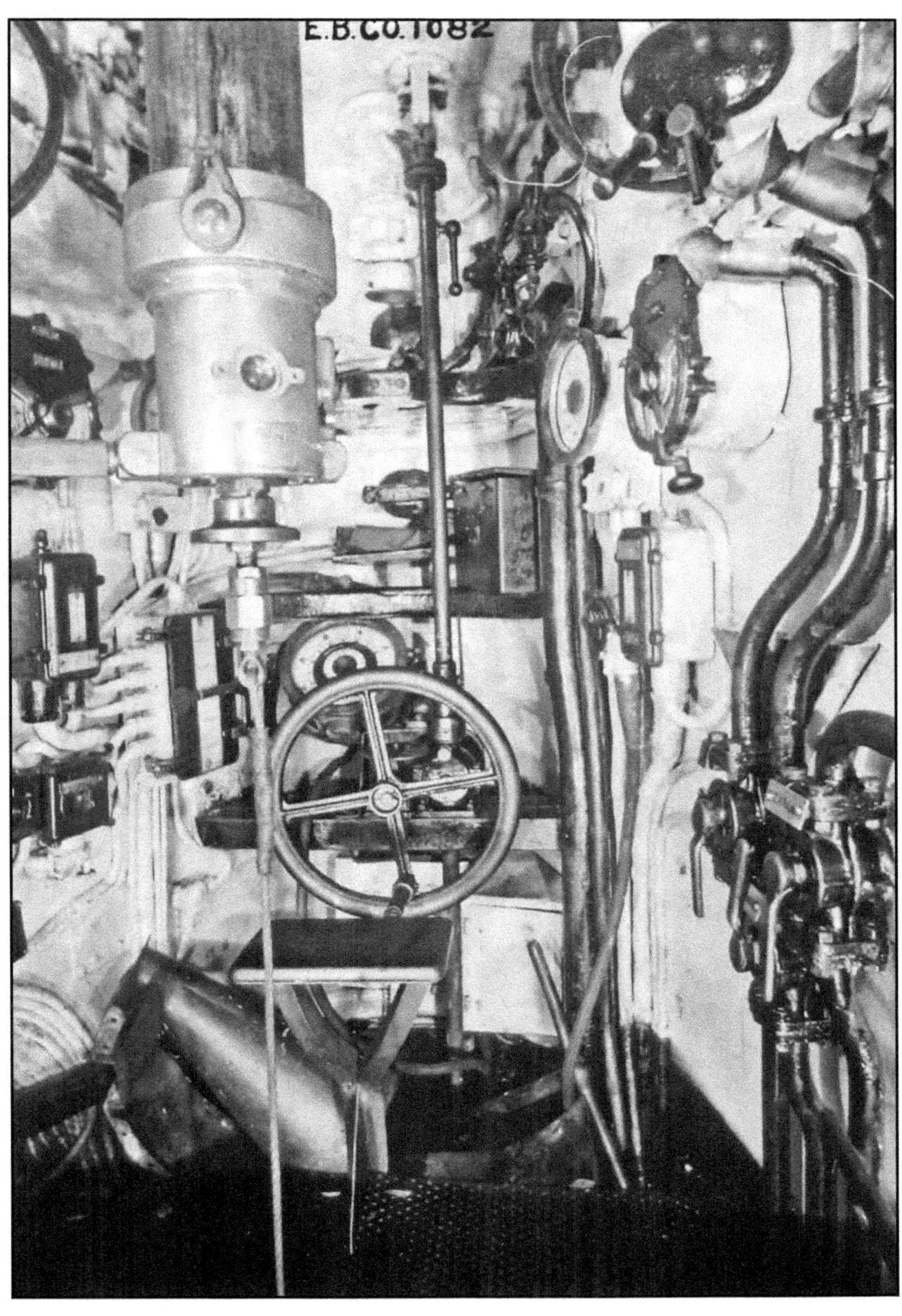

E.B.CO. 1083

E.B.CO.1086

U-111 (From the author's collection)

U-111 (From the author's collection)

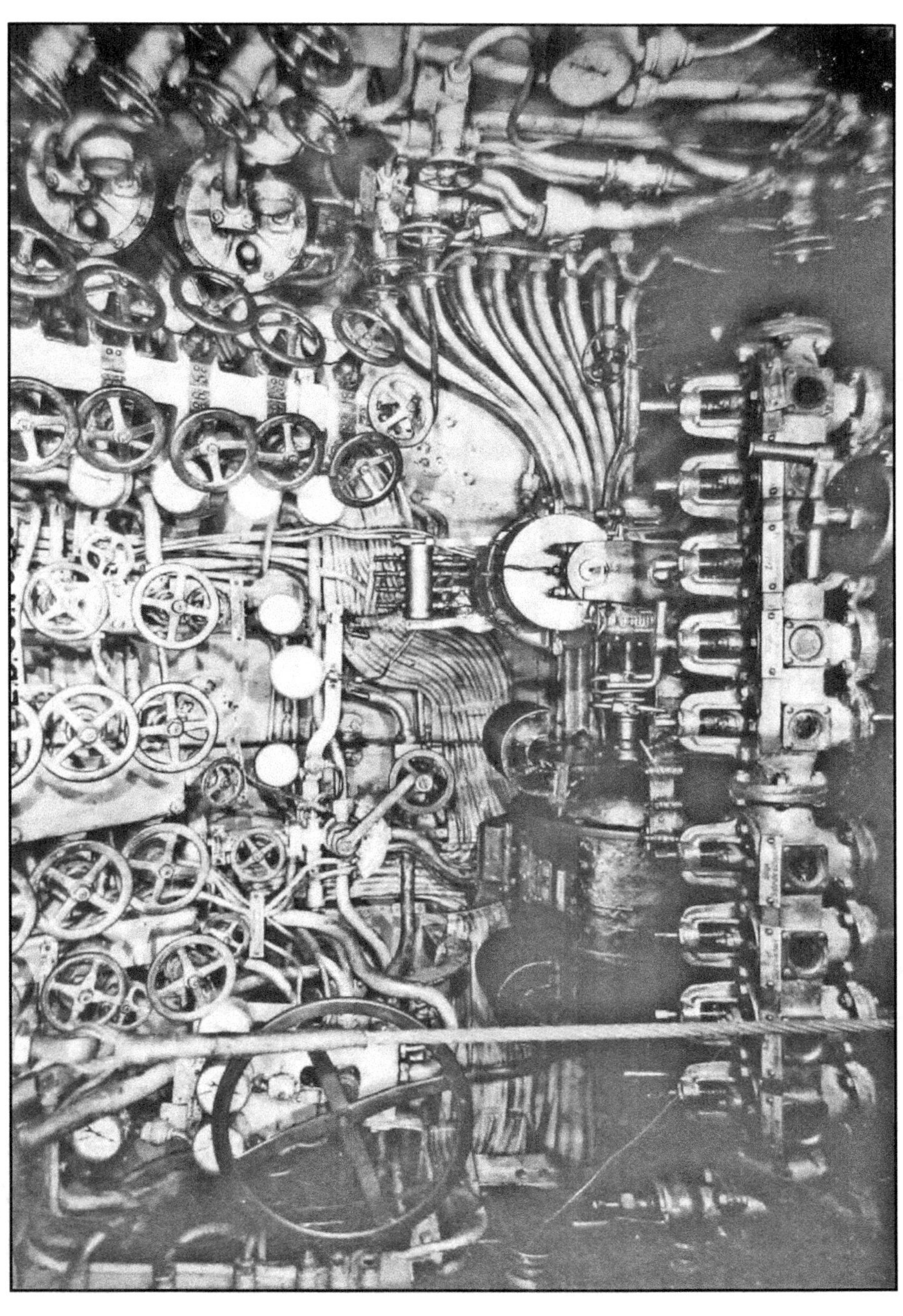

U-111 (From the author's collection)

E.B.CO. 1093

U-111 (From the author's collection)

U-111 (From the author's collection)

U-111 (From the author's collection)

U-111 (From the author's collection)

U-111 (From the author's collection)

U-111 (From the author's collection)

U-111 (From the author's collection)

U-111 (From the author's collection)

F BCD 11104

U-111 (From the author's collection)

U-111 (From the author's collection)

U-111 (From the author's collection)

U-111 (From the author's collection)

U-111 (From the author's collection)

U-111 (From the author's collection)

E.B.CO.1113

U-111 (From the author's collection)

U-111 (From the author's collection)

U-111 (From the author's collection)

U-111 (From the author's collection)

U-111 (From the author's collection)

U-111 (From the author's collection)

The main aisle of my 15,000-volume library.

Two of the three rows that lead off the main aisle.

The U-boat section of my library.

My study with handy reference volumes.

Four of twelve file cabinets, dedicated to shipwreck research.

The Popular Dive Guide Series

Shipwrecks of Maine and New Hampshire
Shipwrecks of Massachusetts: North
Shipwrecks of Massachusetts: South
Shipwrecks of Rhode Island and Connecticut
Shipwrecks of New York
Shipwrecks of New Jersey (1988)
Shipwrecks of New Jersey: North
Shipwrecks of New Jersey: Central
Shipwrecks of New Jersey: South
Shipwrecks of Delaware and Maryland (1990 Edition)
Shipwrecks of Delaware and Maryland (2002 Edition)
Shipwrecks of the Chesapeake Bay in Maryland Waters
Shipwrecks of the Chesapeake Bay in Virginia Waters
Shipwrecks of Virginia
Shipwrecks of North Carolina: from the Diamond Shoals North
Shipwrecks of North Carolina: from Hatteras Inlet South
Shipwrecks of South Carolina and Georgia

Shipwreck and Nautical History

Andrea Doria: Dive to an Era
Deep, Dark, and Dangerous: Adventures and Reflections on the Andrea Doria
Great Lakes Shipwrecks: a Photographic Odyssey
The Great Navy Wreck Scam
The Fuhrer's U-boats in American Waters
Ironclad Legacy: Battles of the USS Monitor
The Kaiser's U-boats in American Waters
The Lusitania Controversies: Atrocity of War and a Wreck-Diving History (Book One)
The Lusitania Controversies: Dangerous Descents into Shipwrecks and Law (Book Two)
The Nautical Cyclopedia
NOAA's Ark: the Rise of the Fourth Reich
Paukenschlag, Hardegen, and the SS Octavian
Shadow Divers Exposed: the Real Saga of the U-869
Shipwreck Heresies
The Shipwreck Research Handbook
Shipwreck Sagas
Stolen Heritage: the Grand Theft of the Hamilton and Scourge
Track of the Gray Wolf
The $25 Dollar Wreck of the Robert J. Walker
U-111 Exposed
Underwater Reflections
USS San Diego: the Last Armored Cruiser
Wreck Diving Adventures

Dive Training

Primary Wreck Diving Guide
Advanced Wreck Diving Guide
The Advanced Wreck Diving Handbook
Ultimate Wreck Diving Guide
The Technical Diving Handbook

Nonfiction

The Absurdity Principle
Lehigh Gorge Trail Guide
Lehigh River Paddling Guide
Wilderness Canoeing

Science Fiction

A Different Universe
A Different Dimension
A Different Continuum
Entropy (a novel of conceptual breakthrough)
A Journey to the Center of the Earth
The Mold
Return to Mars
Second Coming
Silent Autumn
Subaqueous
Tesla and the Lemurian Gate
The Time Dragons Trilogy
- *A Time for Dragons*
- *Dragons Past*
- *No Future for Dragons*

Sci-Fi Action/Adventure Novels

Memory Lane
Mind Set
The Peking Papers

Supernatural Horror Novel

The Lurking: Curse of the Jersey Devil

Vietnam Novel

Lonely Conflict

Videotape or DVD

The Battle for the USS Monitor

Visit the GGP website for availability of titles:
http://www.ggentile.com

Of the thousands of decompression dives that Gary Gentile has made, 200 of them were on the Grand Dame of the Sea: the *Andrea Doria.* In 1990, he merged mixed-gas diving technology with wreck-diving, in order to dive on the German battleship *Ostfriesland*, which lay at a depth of 380 feet. In 1994, he participated in a mixed-gas diving expedition to the *Lusitania*, at 300 feet.

Gary has specialized in wreck-diving and shipwreck research, concentrating his efforts on wrecks along the eastern seaboard, from Newfoundland to Dry Tortugas, and in the Great Lakes. He has compiled an extensive library of books, photographs, drawings, plans, and original source materials on ships and shipwrecks.

Gary has written scores of magazine articles, and has published more than 4,000 photographs in books, periodicals, newspapers, brochures, advertisements, corporate reports, museum displays, postcards, film, and television. He lectures extensively on wilderness and underwater topics, and conducts seminars on advanced wreck-diving techniques, high-tech diving equipment, and wreck photography. He is the author of more than five dozen books: primarily science fiction novels and non-fiction works on diving and on nautical and shipwreck history. The Popular Dive Guide Series will eventually cover every major shipwreck along the east coast of the United States.

Gary has discovered and/or identified more than 40 shipwrecks.

In 1989, after a five-year battle with the National Oceanic and Atmospheric Administration, Gary won a suit which forced the hostile government agency to issue him a permit to dive the USS *Monitor*, a protected National Marine Sanctuary. Media attention that was focused on Gary's triumphant victory resulted in nationwide coverage of his 1990 photographic expedition to the Civil War ironclad. Gary continues to fight for the right of access to all shipwreck sites.

From the author's collection.

From Rustin Cassway <rcassway@demount.com>
To gary@ggentile.com <gary@ggentile.com>
Date 2022-11-07 13:58
Priority Highest

Gary,

Thanks for your e-mail.

The facts are:

You were 100% the first to suggest that R8 was U-111. Your 30 year old Virginia Book also has the U-111 4 miles from the numbers.

With continues warmest regards

Rusty

This is an excerpt from a personal email that Cassway sent to me. I edited the text for clarity by folding the print-out. This edited version in no way takes his declarations out of context. I am not a good folder.

www.ingramcontent.com/pod-product-compliance
Lightning Source LLC
LaVergne TN
LVHW020051110826
845155LV00021B/65